BECOMING
EFFECTIVE FATHERS
AND MENTORS

BY SHELDON D. NIX

A WORKBOOK THAT PREPARES BLACK MEN
TO BE FATHERS AND MENTORS

BECOMING EFFECTIVE FATHERS AND MENTORS
by Sheldon D. Nix
Edited by Eugene Seals
Designed by Cheryl Blum
Cover Photo by Wendy Nelson, Blue Fox Photography

Printed in the United States of America.

Published by Cook Communications Ministries, Colorado Springs, CO 80918, and Renaissance Productions, Woodbury, NJ 08096.

ISBN 0-7814-5317-8

BECOMING EFFECTIVE FATHERS AND MENTORS

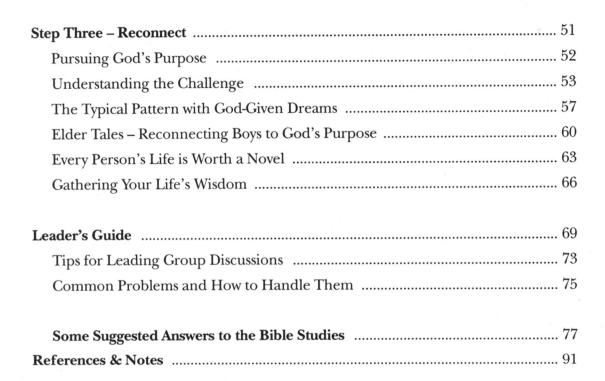

WHY SHARE MY LIFE?

In 1989, I was awakened to the plight of African American males by Rev. E. K. Bailey of Dallas, Texas, founder of one of the earliest ministries to black men. Rev. Bailey called for a special outreach to black males. In response, I began formulating a strategy called Project Manhood to reach black male college students while I served as National Director of Black Campus Ministries with InterVarsity Christian Fellowship, USA.

I next became the founding director of a hospital-based community outreach center in Camden, New Jersey, ranked by the U. S. Conference of Mayors as one of the four most distressed cities in America. There I translated my ideas into a comprehensive model program focused on 8- to 13-year-old boys. Project Manhood has seven basic components:

> • Manhood Training, in which boys are taught the values, habits, attitudes, and skills of "authentic" men;
> • Peer Resistance & Dysfunctional Behavior Prevention Training, in which boys are taught peer resistance and other skills to prevent dysfunctional behaviors such as violence, drug addiction, and

premarital sex;
> • Counseling & Case Management, in which laymen provide boys with problem-solving counseling and ensure that their various needs get met through community resources;
> • Career Development & Entrepreneurial Training, in which boys are helped to career maturity and are taught to develop small businesses of their own;
> • Mentoring, Academic Achievement and Parent Training. These components are under development at this time.

A separate curriculum will address parent training.

The Project Manhood curriculum, *Let the Journey Begin,* the first of its kind, draws psychological principles from the life of Joseph in the Old Testament to teach boys how to be men. It focuses on the values, attitudes, habits, and skills fundamental to becoming a man and is available now from Cook Communications.

What I have found is that many men are reluctant to mentor their sons or other boys because of a deep sense of personal inadequacy for the task. They have the interest. But they don't feel like they can do an adequate job of helping their boys become the men God intended them to become. This is a serious wound we have suffered in our development as individuals and as a people.

Like the other manuals I have developed, *Becoming Effective Fathers and Mentors* is biblically based and psychologically sound. It draws on some of the most up-to-date approaches to helping African American men overcome the deep wounds they have suffered in their lives. It prepares the emotional ground for them to nurture black boys to manhood. It is not a parenting manual or a how-to mentoring manual. Rather, it prepares men to feel able to parent and/or mentor; it helps them overcome the emotional blocks to wanting to be a father or mentor, blocks I encountered as director of the men's ministry in my church.

You Have a Life to Pass On — What a Man Can Give a Boy

As a minister, psychologist, and social worker, I already knew the statistics concerning African American men and the tragedy that occurs every day in large portions of the African American family – the physical or emotional absence of the father. But as each man in the men's ministry in our church shared his image of his father, I was still stunned at the disappointment and pain on the faces of the men. The session was entitled "Finding Our Fathers," and I had asked each man to share with the others what his image was of his father. Although our church was located in one of America's poorest cities, our men represented a wide range of income and occupational levels. Yet, regardless of station in life, for all but two of us, the image of our fathers was negative – our dads had been either physically absent or psychologically unavailable during our crucial developmental years.

One man, in particular, stands out. "Ted" (not his real name) at the time was in his late twenties. Ted's father had moved out of the family home and had begun

...THE ABSENCE OF A FATHER IN HIS LIFE HAD CREATED A VACUUM...

another family when Ted was still in his early teens. Ted began to cry as he expressed his hurt and anger over a father who, he said, gave the other woman's children far more time and attention than he had given Ted and his siblings. "If my father had given me guidance," Ted speculated painfully, "maybe I wouldn't have gotten into some of the things I did." Ted was referring, for one thing, to his walk down the path of drug addiction. Well into his recovery at this point and an emerging church leader, he sensed as he searched his inner self that the lack of fatherly guidance, the absence of a father in his life, had created a vacuum that he had filled any way he could. It had created a self-destructive process that he had only recently begun to turn around.

Ted was a man with a "father wound." Many of us have made the passage into adulthood handicapped by inadequate fathering. Our fathers were physically absent from the family home and from our lives to a significant degree; or they were psychologically absent, unavailable to give us the intimacy and nurturing that we needed.

THE HOLE AT THE CENTER OF AFRICAN AMERICAN MEN

In our hearts, there is a hole where there should be memories of a loving father watching over us, teaching us, guiding us, protecting us, and praising us. For so many African American men there is instead a silence, an emptiness. No father memories fill our minds; or what father memories we have are negative, filled with pain and anger. There is a gap in our souls that our fathers were supposed to fill.

This gap is also growing in the lives of African American boys today. They do not have men in their lives who can tell them and show them what it means to be a man. They have no living examples to show them how a boy can make the long journey to manhood.

Becoming Effective Fathers and Mentors is a workbook to help you become a man who can stand in the gap, a man who can fill the silence in our boys' hearts with the wisdom you have gained from your life. Yes, you have much wisdom to share with our boys, more than you now realize. No matter how twisted and difficult your own journey to manhood has been, no matter how many false trails you have followed – on your journey you have seen much and heard much and learned much that can help a boy become a man.

Like most of us, however, you are broken in many areas of your life. You have deep wounds that have not healed, perhaps wounds you are not even aware of. I know, for while I am a psychologist and an ordained Baptist minister, I am also a broken man. The wounds in my own soul run deep. Some of them are taking a long time to heal. I, too, have wandered far and wide in my journey to manhood. Even now, my trail is steep and very, very difficult.

But wounds can heal. We can recover from the wounds this world has given us. There is an example in the story of Moses. Moses is much like many of us. He came from a broken home, raised without his own father, raised by strong women. He was raised with a sense of purpose and destiny, but the world broke him. For forty years he stayed broken and wounded until God came looking for him to recover him, rebuild him, and re-connect him with God's purpose for Moses' life so that Moses in turn could reconnect the children of Israel with God's purpose for their lives.

THE ROLE OF A FATHER OR MENTOR

Before we dig into the story of how Moses was broken and then recovered, I want to discuss why a boy needs a man. From my studies and observations, there are nine critical things a man can give a boy that a woman cannot give him in the way he needs them:

1. PROVIDE HIM WITH A FEELING OF SAFETY.

When we are scared as young children – either by external dangers such as strangers or by internal dangers such as dreams of monsters – we need someone big and strong to comfort us and tell us that we are safe. As we grow older, when we are scared we will call on those memories of being comforted by dad and remind ourselves that dad said we are okay. Soon enough, we will be able to comfort ourselves.

But what happens when a boy grows up with no one there to really make him feel safe? What happens when the father who is around is emotionally absent and, therefore, doesn't make the boy feel safe? In some cases, a father may be around but may even make a boy feel unsafe, as in the case of an extremely angry, abusive, and/or alcoholic man. Many boys grow up today without a positive father memory to draw on when they are feeling unsafe.

2. IMPOSE LIMITS.

A boy needs limits set for him. He needs to know what is right and what is wrong. He needs to be made to do his homework when he would rather play or watch television. These limits should not be excessively strict, but they do need to be there. As Jawanza Kunjufu points out, a time will come when a boy will test the limits. If there is no strong man there to enforce those limits, the boy is likely to cross them and never come back. After a while, mothers generally lose control of their sons. Sometimes, they even become afraid of them. Boys need a man "big" enough to enforce limits without using violence.

3. PROMOTE INDEPENDENCE.

If you always need your actual parents around you to get you to function – whether brushing your teeth before bed or studying before you go out to play or the like – then you are not independent. As you grow up, you are supposed to learn to set limits for yourself. So many boys grow up passive and dependent on mom – and later on their peers – to dictate their behavior because they never had a man to really promote their independence. They have no father image to draw on. When they are afraid to take a risk and apply for a better job, there is no memory of a father telling them in their minds, "I believe in you, Son. Go for it. You've got what it takes." Unless someone takes them by the hand down to the interview, they won't go. Some boys need a man, not so much to set limits, but to get the boy to be confident enough in himself to be independent. (Watch out for boys who seem to be independent simply because they won't listen to their mothers. Often, they have just shifted their dependency to their peer group or gang!)

4. SERVE AS A MODEL FOR CHARACTER DEVELOPMENT.

We are well aware today of the importance of role models. How else can we determine what being a man is unless we have seen some models? Too many boys grow up without such models or with poor ones. A woman can tell a boy what a man is, but cannot show him. You don't have to be perfect, only growing as a man.

5. PROMOTE DEVELOPMENT OF A CONSCIENCE.

Our parents teach us about right and wrong. This helps develop our conscience. What is fascinating about this is that women and men think differently about moral issues. A lot of research shows this. Men have one way of thinking about things. Women have another. No wonder an adolescent boy stops trusting his mother's thoughts about morality. She doesn't speak his language. It's too feminine for him. He needs to be exposed to a man's conscience, a man's way of solving problems and handling moral questions.

6. PROVIDE AN IDEAL SELF.

Our ideal self is the man we want to be. What we want to become, the goals we have for ourselves, the way we ideally would like to live our lives determines what our lives become. As we grow up trying to get a picture of this "ideal me," we look around at the men in our lives and pick and choose the traits we want to have for ourselves. Haven't you noticed young children staring at people? They are looking at how others behave, at what happens when people behave as they do. Over time, they make decisions about what they want to be.

> **A BOY NEEDS A MAN TO HELP HIM DEVELOP AN IDEAL SELF**

A boy needs a man to help him develop an ideal self of which he will one day be proud. Without real men around to use as models, he will only have television men – unreal men who are usually white – and sports heroes, who don't show their real selves. And he will have his peer group, who aren't men at all.

7. HELP HIM SEPARATE FROM MOTHER.

A father or mentor can help a boy separate from his mother and the world of women and identify with the world of men (and find his own woman)! But many boys today have no father to help them make this separation. They remain too much under their mother's influence long into adulthood and thus fail to achieve their full manhood. Or they try to separate from mother too soon, on their own or through a male peer group. This usually leads to behavior problems such as acting out, drugs, and gangs since a boy needs a man's help in smoothly becoming a separate, adult man.

8. BE A "MIRROR" OF WHO HE IS BECOMING.

To be a mirror is to help someone see himself clearly in a way he cannot without the mirror. A boy needs a man to help him see how he is doing as he is growing to manhood. "Oh, Johnny, look how strong you are," someone may say when Johnny pushes a large (for him) piece of furniture. "You did very poorly on this test, Daryl, because you are not concentrating on your work." Daryl knows he did poorly, because the teacher told him so. But his "mirror" told him why. It is not because he is stupid, as he might start to think without the mirror, but because he didn't try hard enough. If he is stupid in his mind, then his ideal self will not let him strive for academic excellence

because he feels that stupid people can't be academically excellent. He will shoot for being mediocre or will turn his attention to sports or some other positive or negative area of achievement. But if a mirror tells him that his failure had to do with lack of effort, that is a cause he can do something about.

Our boys don't have enough black male mirrors. They have white mirrors – their teachers – who may or may not give them a true reflection of themselves. They have the television mirror, which gives them all kinds of distorted views of themselves. They have law enforcement mirrors sometimes – which tell them not that they are sons of kings and children of the King of kings, but criminals, thugs, worthless, dangerous garbage. They need strong black male mirrors who can ultimately point them to the One who created them and knows them better than they know themselves.

9. Show him how to survive as an African American man in a racist society.

Our boys get quickly overwhelmed by the racism and discrimination in this country. Perhaps in your own journey, you, too, have been driven off your path by the winds of rejection, prejudice, unfair treatment, or last hired/first fired practices. But you can still talk to him about our history as a people and how we have struggled to gain our rightful place in this society. You can talk to him about his dignity as a man created by God, for whom Jesus Christ died. You can teach him how to overcome through committing himself to God's purposes for his

life. You may only be a few steps ahead of him, but that will be enough if you, too, are seeking God's purposes for your own life. None of us have made it. But, like Paul, we "press on toward the prize." We press on together as black men, pressing on against terrible obstacles because we, too, have "the high calling of God in Christ Jesus" (Philippians 3:14).

PASSING ON YOUR LIFE

If you accept the challenge to play this kind of role in a boy's life and give him these nine things whether he is your son or someone else's son, then you will have done something for him no woman can do equally well, something that will last him a lifetime. You don't have to do it forever, just for enough years until he can begin to acquire these things for himself.

But before you can pass on your life effectively, you must heal from your own wounds. The hole in the center of your heart has to be filled by the One who promises to be a Father to the fatherless. Please note that this workbook is best done in a group – because God uses other men to help heal us. We can share our insights and our struggles and pray for each other. You can use this workbook on your own in your own private times with yourself and your God, but I strongly suggest getting with at least one other man and going through your workbooks together.

Now let us begin our journey to recovery, rebuilding, and reconnection.

STEP ONE — RECOVER

Moses is a good example of what God can do in the life of a man. To fully appreciate how God recovered Moses, we must first understand how he was broken. As we examine what broke Moses, we will look at what is breaking us. Then we will look at the recovery process God used with Moses.

Two things broke Moses:
- An outer world designed to dominate and
- An inner world not prepared to handle real life.

We'll look at this outer world first, drawing on Exodus 1. We'll then look at his inner world, drawing on Exodus 2. Finally, we'll look at the recovery process, drawing on Exodus 3.

THE OUTER WORLD THAT BROKE MOSES – A DOMINATION SYSTEM

EXODUS 1

To understand the outer world of Moses and our own outer world as African American men, we have to understand what Professor Walter Wink of Auburn Theological Seminary calls "the Domination System." Wink has written some of the best books on the market on what the Bible calls the Principalities and Powers:

> • *Naming the Powers: The Language of Power in the New Testament* (1984);
>
> • *Unmasking the Powers: The Invisible Forces That Determine Human Existence* (1986); and
>
> • *Engaging the Powers: Discernment and Resistance in a World of Domination* (1992).

The goal of the principalities and powers is to dominate or destroy. As John 10:10 tells us, Satan's purpose is to "kill, steal, and destroy." The whole world is captured by a system of lies, delusions, and institutions which all work together to promote the domination of people and to prevent them from embracing their Creator and Savior. The Bible uses the Greek word cosmos, which usually means "world system." It is a system of institutions and beliefs which seeks to destroy the good world God created.

Where do we see the principalities and powers at work? Consider the following wide range of endeavors that encompass every area in which you and I may be involved.

THE WORLD DOMINATION SYSTEM	**HOW CHRISTIANS ARE INFLUENCED BY IT**
IN POLITICS: We see conquest, authoritarian leaders, manipulation, and deceit – all so that the powerful can control.	Have you seen a church battle lately? Over the budget? Over whether to throw the pastor out? Over whether to get new carpeting? It can get pretty ugly, as people seek to dominate each other.
IN ECONOMICS: We see exploitation, greed, privilege, and inequality.	Have you noticed how often those who have lots of wealth give a smaller percentage of their income to the church than those of lesser means? Research has shown that the higher the income, the less generous people tend to be. It is easier for a camel to go through the eye of a needle. . . .
IN RELATIONSHIPS: We often see some people on top, others on the bottom in an "us vs. them" battle. In such "domination hierarchies" (Wink), we see injustice, abuse, anger, deceit.	In the Christian community, there are many negative hierarchies – some people on top trying to control others or put them down. Often our relationships do not demonstrate the selfless love of Christ, but instead prove our own brokenness as people.
IN ECOLOGY: We see contempt for the earth, a desire to exploit natural resources instead of preserving the home in which we all have to live.	Christians don't do a better job of caring for the earth than the world does. If anything, we recycle even less than they do. We litter as much as anyone. We don't conserve energy. We don't fight to save God's earth.

THE WORLD DOMINATION SYSTEM	HOW CHRISTIANS ARE INFLUENCED BY IT

IN EDUCATION: We see indoctrination – telling kids and adults what to think, instead of teaching people to think for themselves and challenge the ways people have thought in the past.

We also see some people getting a better education than others.

Christian schools and Bible institutes often indoctrinate even worse than secular schools (because the teachers/pastors believe they have *the* correct interpretation of the Bible). If people don't believe the official doctrines, they are often put down. Christian teachers/pastors often lecture instead of teaching people how to intensively study the Bible for themselves.

IN THE PRINCIPLES BY WHICH WE LIVE: Colossians 2:8, 20, and Galatians 4:3, 9 talk about the "elementary principles," the "rudiments," and "beggarly elements" of the world system. These fundamental principles by which the world runs are contrary to the truth of God. What are they? Here are some examples adapted from Dr. Wink:

• To prevent chaos, you have to control people – dominate them.

• Doesn't this happen in the church when we try to force people to believe what we believe and to live the way we think they should live? Do we really set them free to be guided by our mutual Lord?

• Men are better equipped to be dominant than women. Some races are created to dominate others.

• Does the Bible really call for men to dominate women? We know it doesn't teach that whites are supposed to dominate the earth. Nonetheless, look how many Christians are part of the international white power structures that oppress people around the world.

THE WORLD DOMINATION SYSTEM	**HOW CHRISTIANS ARE INFLUENCED BY IT**
• Only the fittest have the right to survive. If you fall, you deserve it.	• What do we do in the Christian community when a brother falls? Don't we often judge him instead of restoring him? It has been said that the Church is the only army that shoots its wounded.
• Those who rule have a right to extra privileges.	• How do we treat our pastors? Many of us who do not put them on a pedestal and treat them as kings go to the opposite extreme and tend to tear them down.
• Money and property are a sign and proof of your political and social worth. If you have it, you deserve to rule. In fact, you should make as much as you can. You deserve it.	• Look how many Christians believe that money and property are signs of God's blessing, despite all the references in the Bible that put God on the side of the poor.

The world's principles can be so subtle. We can be living by them and not even be aware of it! We've been "bewitched," as Paul told the Galatians, lured back into living by the "beggarly elements" that never saved us in the first place! The clue is to look and see if we are guilty of (1) dominating or destroying anyone or (2) allowing people to be dominated or destroyed by the system (including the church system).

Everywhere we look, we can see the biblical truth that the "Prince of this world" (John 12:31) has established a whole system by which people are dominated – or, if they won't play ball, by which they are destroyed. It doesn't take a demon to wreak havoc by attacking every individual on earth. (There aren't enough to go around!) The Prince of this world has set the whole world system up to dominate or destroy people and to keep them from their Lord.

So what we find in Egypt in Moses' day is just one small part of the world domination system, one small manifestation of the principalities and powers. Pharaoh's goal was to set up a slavery system that would break the Hebrews. The Bible says, "So the Egyptians made the children of Israel serve with rigor" (Exodus 1:13, NKJV). The Hebrew word translated "rigor" means "to break apart." The Hebrews "waxed exceedingly mighty" (Exodus 1:7, KJV), accumulating houses and land and businesses. So a system was designed to break apart their families, farms, and businesses so that Egypt could dominate them.

The same thing happened to African American men. The British-American system of slavery was deliberately designed to break the manhood of the Africans. From the moment they got the Africans in chains, the slave catchers – and later the slave masters – set out to break the spirit of the slaves, especially the men. Any show of defiance, of spirit, of manhood, was met with brutal force. They were packed in slave ships like sardines to make them believe the delusion that they were not human beings but instruments, tools, property. In America, they had no rights.

Today, the Domination System, the principalities and powers, succeed in stripping away our manhood in many different ways. You are now going to explore how your own manhood has been wounded, perhaps deeply, by a System which was set up before you were born and whose purpose is to destroy you as a man.

In the space provided in the oval below:

1. Describe the social, political, and economic pressures the Egyptians put on the Hebrew men. (What social, political, and economic forces made life more difficult for them? Remember, before Pharaoh put this pressure on them, they were wealthy, independent businessmen and landowners running their own lives and communities.)

2. Describe the social, political, and economic support God provided that the Hebrew men could draw on to make their lives more bearable.

3. Describe the pressures the Egyptian Domination System put on the Hebrew family (Exodus 1:16, 22).

4. Describe the support God provided to the Hebrew families (1:17-20).

THE EGYPTIAN DOMINATION SYSTEM

THE PRESSURES EGYPT USED TO DOMINATE

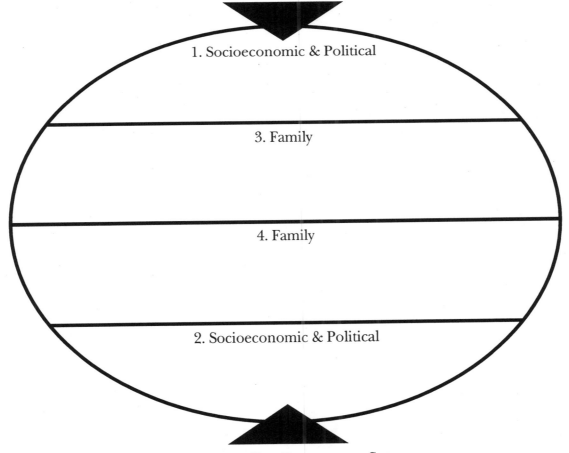

1. Socioeconomic & Political

3. Family

4. Family

2. Socioeconomic & Political

THE SUPPORT GOD PROVIDED TO SUSTAIN

In the space provided in the oval below:

1. Describe the social, political, and economic pressures that the principalities and powers are putting on you. (What social, political, and economic forces make life more difficult for you?)

2. Describe the social, political, and economic support God is providing you to make your life more bearable.

3. Describe the pressures the Domination System you live under is putting on your family (either a family you created by marriage or whatever group of people is your support system, your "family substitute").

4. Describe the support God is providing to your "family".

5. Outside the oval, write a brief statement about how you feel these pressures and supports are affecting you.

THE DOMINATION SYSTEM YOU LIVE IN

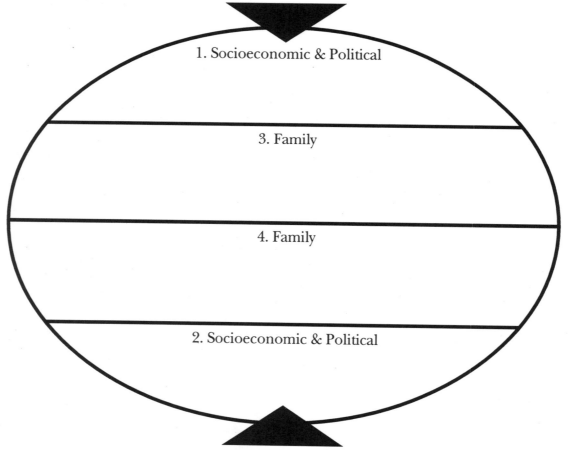

THE PRESSURES BEING USED TO DOMINATE YOU

1. Socioeconomic & Political

3. Family

4. Family

2. Socioeconomic & Political

THE SUPPORT GOD PROVIDES TO SUSTAIN

The Inner World that Broke Moses - A Failed Hero Quest

Exodus 2

"We live in a time of fallen heroes," Drs. Betcher and Pollack tell us:

> The monuments built of men, by men, and for men have tumbled. Men have not just been brought to earth, their strength put in perspective by their flaws. Even their virtues are suspect vices: power has turned out to be oppression; strength, rigidity, and self-sufficiency an inability to be emotionally close. . . . If men still appear in control, their smug certainty is gone. It is a difficult time to be proud of being a man.

What does it mean to be a man during these times of change and turmoil, when the definitions and images of masculinity are in such upheaval? For what are men looking? What are we seeking to be and to do to express our manhood?

Alfred Adler, one of the founders of modern psychology, long ago discovered that much of our behavior can be explained by what we are striving for, what our life goal is. We are goal-seeking creatures; men especially are goal-oriented. And for many of us men, probably most, that goal is to be a hero.

THE HEROIC MALE

This heroic urge can be seen in so many different ways. If you will pardon his language, Jack Balswick – citing Debra David and Robert Brannon (1976) – points out four major themes in the traditional male heroic role:

- **The Big Wheel** – the degree to which a man achieves in the world of education and work;
- **The Sturdy Oak** – referring to the need of men to be strong, tough, confident, self-reliant;
- **Give 'em Hell!** – referring to the expectation that men be adventurous, daring, aggressive, even violent; and
- **No Sissy Stuff** – the message to men that they avoid being "feminine", that they must not show their feelings; "real" men must not to be soft, vulnerable, uncertain, and the like.

Aaron Kipnis (in *Knights Without Armor*) gives an interesting list of the traits of the heroic, or "hyper-masculine," model of manhood in four major areas below (I've interpreted some of his traits):

- **Physical:** He is hard, dominating, tough, a soldier, a killer, coercive, controlling, lord and master, destructive;
- **Emotional:** He is closed, numb, co-dependent, demanding, aggressive, cynical, a sex partner, defensive, and repressed;
- **Mental:** He is compartmentalized, penetrating, analytical, splitting, linear, hierarchy oriented, exploitive, focused on rules and laws, a doctor who will fix people; and
- **Spiritual:** He is patriarchal (men dominate), black and white in his beliefs, never doubtful, not open to disagreement; single (independent, just me and God), but divided inside (lots of unresolved inner conflicts and doubts that he never lets people know about).

What are men seeking to be? Again, the classic quest is to become a hero. We can see this in two major areas of a man's life: work and women. Success and sex seem to be a man's two basic drives. That is probably only partially true, but it does have a lot of truth to it! Let's look at the quest for success.

THE QUEST FOR SUCCESS

Why are men driven to succeed? There are historic, psychological, and theologi-cal explanations. As society became industrialized, a man's work became separated from his household. He began to go to the factory or office, often far away from home, rather than out to the fields connected to his home. This fostered an increasingly deeper division in society between the domestic, less-respected world of women (the socially intimate world of children, home, and husband) and the public, respected world of men (the less intimate, hierarchical world of societal institutions where achieving goals and dominance over the competition counted). As a result, we have seen that when a man gets out into that tough, cold world of dog-eat-dog competition, his natural tendencies toward dominance and achievement get multiplied ten-fold. He either produces or he's going to get stepped on. His ego is put on the line day after day. So his primary attention gets focused tightly on making it.

Taking the psychological perspective, we see that men gain their sense of significance from their work. From an early age, men are socialized to consider their primary obligation to be providing for themselves and their families (the Protestant work ethic). The Bible offers a good deal of support for this position, "If a man will not work, he shall not eat" (II Thessalonians 3:10). Further, it may be said that men's orientation toward status, achievement, independence, rationality, and dominance makes the world of work a natural place for them, whereas the fuzzy relational world of the family – in which goals are unclear, where "relating" and "emoting" are primary ways the

game is played – is much more foreign to them.

There may also be a theological explanation for men's high focus on work. When God created Adam, he commanded him to rule the earth. Adam's first tasks involved work of a sort: caring for the garden, naming the animals. Even though the command to exercise dominion over the earth was given to both man and woman, the curse on man involved his work, while the curse on Eve involved her relationships with children and husband. Thus, one might suppose that God cursed men in the precise area of their central focus. Or, putting it differently, God knew that men's primary orientation toward working would bring them their most central challenges and heartaches. Fallen men might then be said to be trying hardest to overcome their central challenge (the thorns and sweat of work). This sense of work as rising to meet a challenge is spoken of by Robert Hicks:

> Many men use work to prove something to themselves, their fathers, or early mentors about their own manhood. . . . They try to prove . . . that they can make it even when those mentors thought they were losers.

The working world is thus the primary testing ground for a man, the battlefield where he strives to prove his manhood.

AFRICAN AMERICAN MEN – UNWANTED HEROES

If work is the primary proving ground for men and career success the proof of manhood, what happens to many (but not all) African American men whose attempts to achieve status are made even more difficult by societal obstacles such as discrimination and inferior school systems? The result can be what Amos Wilson (*Black-on-Black Violence: The Psychodynamics of Black Self-Annihilation in Service of White Domination*) calls "reactionary masculinity." He speaks with graphic directness about the self-destructive behavior that can result from chronic, community-wide powerlessness in generation after generation of African American men:

> Black-on-black violence is reflective of vain attempts to achieve basic, positive human ends in a negative environment by negative means. It represents an often misguided, furious struggle for self-affirmation by many African Americans while entangled in a white American-spun spider's web specifically designed and constructed to accomplish their dis-affirmation. . . . For too many African American youth, being cut off from the paths to legitimate and self-determined personal accomplishment as a result of the underdeveloped power of the African American community,

the violent subduing of others may often be their only significant achievement and "claim to fame."

Wilson argues strongly that young males' black-on-black violence is the imitation of the violence they see all around them in American society, both physical violence and socioeconomic violence (the American Domination System).

The result is a sense of manhood built around humiliation and rage. In its truest sense, it is "reactionary masculinity." Violence is one reaction. Drug and alcohol abuse is another. Giving up the male quest for success is yet another, resulting in a lasting sense of shame about being a failure as a man. By giving up the struggle, these boys and men don't have to risk their deeply wounded self-esteem any further. After all, no one can reject you for a job for which you didn't apply or criticize you for a test which you didn't bother to take.

But even if, as black men or as black boys, we have given up the quest for success, we deep down still want to be successful. So we feel badly about ourselves and take it out on each other or on ourselves.

And this is precisely what happened with Moses. His own hero quest failed, as you will see, and he took it out on himself. Take a minute to answer the following questions:

THE FALL OF MOSES

1. Childhood Upbringing: What effect do you think Moses' being a Hebrew and separated from his parents (raised in a "foster home") had on him? (Consider only Exodus 2 and Acts 7:28.

_____

_____

2. What effect do you think Moses' being raised an Egyptian prince had on his psychological mindset? (Hint: Think about his self-esteem and his sense of destiny.)

_____

_____

3. What do we learn about the character and mindset of Moses in Exodus 2:11-14 and Acts 7:25?

_____

_____

4. Given his background, what was the psychological impact on Moses of the life crisis (life failure) described in Exodus 2:13-15?

_____

_____

5. Given everything that had happened to him, why would Moses agree to stay in the Midian desert for 40 years, giving up his hero quest to free his people (Exodus 2:21)? (Hint: Think of what he was running from and what he got from the land of Midian.)

_____

_____

A few comments are in order before we look at the sixth question. Midian is that place to which we flee for safety. It is not where God wants us to be. It does not allow us to advance his kingdom. As Christians, we are – like Moses – aliens there (see Exodus 4:22). We don't really belong there. We often live in hiding. Our attempt to be a hero – to find success and sex/love – has failed. So we compromise and accept what gives us some good feelings, some degree of happiness, a measure of safety, or a morsel of peace.

Perhaps our Midian is an alcohol bottle where we try to numb our pain and sorrows. It may be an obsession with watching TV sports or working non-stop at our job instead of spending time with our lady or with our children. We feel more comfortable dealing with sports and work than with intimacy. It may be that we are hiding our hurt behind our anger. It is easier to let people (especially other men) see our anger, our macho, our "big, bad attitude," than to let them see that we are hurt, vulnerable, and needy. So we only show the safe part of our feelings – our tough, angry side. It may be giving up on finishing our degree. ("I don't need any more school. I have too much to do trying to make it.") It could be some hard-to-let-go-of sin. It could be any number of other compromises and rationalizations which we put forth in an attempt to deceive ourselves and others while artificially bolstering our self-esteem.

Midian is where we hide and try to build some kind of life for ourselves. It is not our dream. It is not that "ideal self" we talked about earlier. But it is safe and we can be more or less successful at it.

6. In privacy, list the "Midians" in your life – the ways you hide from your own hero quest and God's purposes for your life. (Group leaders, on this question ask men to verbalize ONLY what they feel comfortable sharing, if anything. Give them permission to reflect silently if they prefer.)

AN AUTHORITY ISSUE?

Another way of looking at what happened to cause Moses to fall is to see that he had a problem with his sense of responsibility and with authority. He was raised to feel bold, confident, and in charge, with the authority to make things happen the way he wanted them to. After all, he was a prince of Egypt. But he forgot a very important fact. His authority was not absolute. He received his authority from a higher authority – Pharaoh, the king of Egypt. Moses forgot that he would lose that

Some men do not take enough authority or responsibility for their lives.

Their language is filled with blaming other people for what has happened to them. They feel helpless to make the changes or reach the goals they have for their families, for relationships, for their personal lives, and so forth. They don't really feel deep down inside that God can help them change. They give up.

authority once he stepped out from under Pharaoh's authority.

Like African American boys today, Moses was born at a time when there was a campaign to destroy his people's manhood by destroying their boys. Pharaoh – feeling threatened by the success of the Hebrew people – stripped them of their possessions and rights, put them under bondage, and ordered all newly born Hebrew boys killed. The Hebrew mothers and midwives, with God's assistance, did what they could to keep the boys alive, much as African American mothers have done. Still there were very many casualties.

This situation of bondage and danger made it very difficult to grow up into a responsible, confident Hebrew man. How can anyone feel proud of his manhood when he is treated like an animal and does not have the freedom to govern his own life? The destiny God gave men through Adam to exercise authority in this world under His authority was stolen from the Hebrew men. They had to obey their human masters, not God. At any time, their wives might be raped, their homes violated, and the men could do nothing about it. In a similar way, American society has done its best to steal the God-given destiny from African American men as well. So many of us have been stripped of our sense of responsibility for our lives. We feel powerless. We feel badly about ourselves. We would rather not try than try and fail. The Domination System has won. We are dominated men, many of us.

But God is working in our lives to bring us to a place of confidence and boldness in our authority under His authority.

Put an **X** at the place on the line which represents where you think you are:

TOO LITTLE RESPONSIBILITY   **TOO MUCH RESPONSIBILITY**

> Other men take too much authority or responsibility.
>
> These men feel guilty for things over which they had no control. They are harsh with themselves for not achieving standards that they probably don't have the ability to reach. They always feel on the spot, having to prove themselves through their own efforts. They tend to feel responsible for how other people feel and act (people such as their children, their wives, their subordinates) when in fact they have only limited control over those persons. This can lead them toward a dominance lifestyle. Like Moses, they may act rashly, overconfidently going too far out on a limb, thinking they can stand. But they are ready for a fall.

1. Think about your own childhood and especially your important relationships (mother, father, brothers, sisters, teachers, coach, friends) and memorable experiences (such as school, things you did with friends, and family times). What things prepared you to be responsible for your life? What things taught you confidence in your ability to make a difference in your world? What things gave you a belief in your authority to try to fulfill your purpose and goals?

a. _____
_____
_____

b. _____
_____
_____

c. _____
_____
_____

2. Now think once again. Try to identify the things that robbed you of a sense of responsibility and confidence in your ability to make a difference. (Perhaps you were never allowed the freedom other kids had to go out. Perhaps you were never given any chores for which you were responsible. Perhaps the person who raised you never helped you to think for yourself and make up your own mind about things. Perhaps you made a choice to drop out of school and hang out with the boys.)

a. _____
_____
_____

b. _____
_____
_____

c. _____
_____
_____

3. In what areas of your life today is it most difficult for you to take appropriate (not too little and not too much) authority and responsibility for your life. Describe what is difficult about these areas:

Your Body _____

_____

Sexual Thoughts and Behavior _____

_____

Career Goals _____

_____

Family Life _____

_____

Friendships_____

_____

Spiritual Life _____

_____

Church _____

_____

Community _____

_____

Other _____

_____

THE RECOVERY OF BROKEN MEN

EXODUS 3

I addressed 200 African American Christian men at the end of a three day conference. My session was entitled "Healing the Father Wound." The men had heard from a number of other speakers. It was now my task to lead them into a healing experience with the Father God. I instructed them to close their eyes. "If during this conference," I asked, "while you listened to the various speakers exhorting you to be a certain kind of man – if you felt at any point a sense of shame, a feeling like you wanted to hide – raise your hand."

Approximately 180 hands went up – a phenomenal 90 percent!

The roots of shame in men are deep, especially among African American men, and even more so among African American men who are trying to take seriously the call to biblical manhood. I have come to the conclusion that shame is a central driving force that is at the heart of much of male behavior.

I know whereof I speak. Recently I began a personal exercise of looking back over my own life – at the choices I've made, at the man I've become – and I am not pleased. I wept in shame before the Lord as I realized how many bad choices I have made and continue to make, despite what for me has been a very long-term commitment to Christ. I have come to realize how so much of what I have attempted to do has achieved no lasting good. Many of my efforts have had more to do with my male ego and my hero quest than with the Christ I thought I was serving. I have had important relationships go sour. I am, in many ways, still a broken man.

The pain and shame of these realizations have been the most intense I have ever experienced, nearly unbearable at times. It pains me even more to know that I am not alone, that so many other men can also look back and similarly regret many of their choices and responses. Sooner or later we are forced by life and by God to confront who we really are, and the outcome of that confrontation will determine whether we will become the kind of man God created us to be. The outcome of that self-confrontation will determine whether we pass on our lives effectively to the next generation of African American boys. Likewise, Moses' self-encounter preceded his recovery.

THE RECOVERY OF MOSES

STEP 1: RESTORING INTEREST
Why does God light a fire (Exodus 3:1-4)?

_____

_____

Recovery Principle: How has God lit a fire in your recovery process?

_____

_____

STEP 2: RESTORING SELF-HONESTY
(Exodus 3:4-5)
Why does God tell Moses to take off his shoes? Given that Moses is a broken man with low self-esteem, why is it important for him to have this kind of crisis over who he is? (Hint: Think about the first step in Alcoholics Anonymous and about the first Beatitude.) Is God rubbing a broken man's face in the dirt, or is there something healing about this?

_____

_____

_____

Recovery Principle: What does this teach us about how we men should deal with the shame in our lives? Should we try to hide it? Should we try to hide from it?

_____

_____

STEP 3: RESTORING HOPE
(Exodus 3:6-9)
Why is it important for Moses to know that God is the God of Moses' fathers?

(Hint: Remember that Moses feels like an alien in Midian.)

_____

Why is it important that Moses know what God has seen and heard?

_____

_____

Why is it important for Moses to know what God has decided to do?

_____

_____

Recovery Principle: Where have you lost hope in your own life? How is God restoring it?

_____

_____

_____

STEP 4: RESTORING PURPOSE
(Exodus 3:10-14)
What is the significance of the fact that God called Moses to His service at a broken time in Moses' life, instead of waiting for him to get his life together first?

_____

_____

After forty years in Midian, what does Moses' question reveal about his psychological mindset?

_____

_____

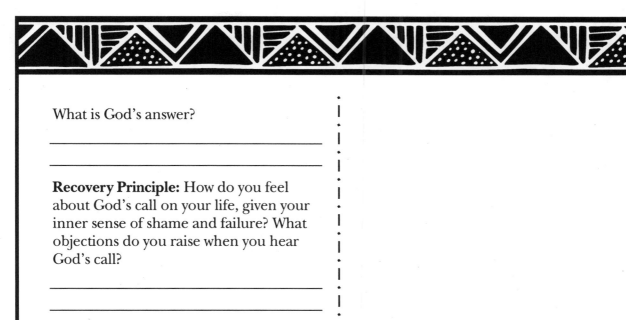

What is God's answer?

_____

_____

Recovery Principle: How do you feel about God's call on your life, given your inner sense of shame and failure? What objections do you raise when you hear God's call?

_____

_____

What is God's answer to you? How does He make that Real? (Don't settle for the "right" answer. Is this really real to you? Why is it real? How would you answer a boy who says God has abandoned him? What reasons that make sense would you give him?)

_____

_____

STEP TWO — REBUILD

EXODUS 3:10 - 4:19

As we have seen, Moses hid in Midian for forty years, deeply discouraged with himself, disillusioned, resigned to raising sheep and a family. His original sense of purpose – that God would use him to deliver his people – had been dashed to pieces. So for forty long years, he gave it up. His whole foundation had been destroyed.

For Moses to become the man God created him to be, he had to be lifted from his discouragement. A new foundation had to be put under his feet. This was not easy. Egypt had shattered Moses' sense of purpose, his sense of self, his sense of authority, his sense of competence, and his sense of connection with his own people and the God of his people.

Many people call these Moses' "complaints." Discouraged men have lost their footing and tend to have a lot of despair and doubts when God first reveals his purpose to them. Rather than be hard on Moses, let us realize that we, too, have our doubts. We, too, have had the rug snatched from under our feet. We, too, have lost our footing, and God has to replace some building blocks in our own foundation. God's anger at Moses was kindled only when Moses resisted God's rebuilding process. Until that point – and even afterward – God graciously placed each building block in position under Moses' feet, stabilizing him and making him ready to fulfill God's purpose for his life.

In the spaces on the following pages, write how God restored each building block in the foundation of Moses' life. Then discuss where you are with each building block. Is it in place? Is it getting in place? Has it not started yet?

33

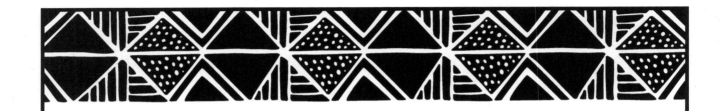

BUILDING BLOCK 1 —
A SENSE OF PURPOSE

Stephen Covey wrote a bestseller called *The Seven Habits of Highly Effective People.* He reviewed the literature of the past 150 years and found that there were seven habits that successful people have in common no matter what area of life represents their success. One of those habits is that they live by principles. They have a deep sense of mission and purpose, and every decision they make is guided by principles they believe will help them achieve their mission.

Tom Peters has written more than one highly regarded book on very successful companies *(In Search of Excellence, Thriving On Chaos).* He found that companies that are highly successful over a long period of time have a very clear purpose and "bone deep beliefs" about how to treat their employees, how to serve their customers, and more. Neither Covey nor Peters emphasizes money. Successful people and companies, they say, focus on principles, on mission, on purpose. The money – or however success is defined – usually follows.

This is very biblical. To be successful in life, you must be a man of purpose. To rebuild the foundation of your life, you have to start with rebuilding your sense of purpose. Should God's man be on a hero's quest? In a way. But for what kind of hero, what kind of ideal self, do you want to strive?

BUILDING BLOCK 1

HOW DOES GOD PUT THIS BLOCK IN PLACE?

SENSE OF PURPOSE
A sense of what God has created me for. "For we are his workmanship, created in Christ Jesus to do good works, which God prepared in advance for us to do" (Ephesians 2:10).

While I have many ideas about my life, I can only be truly successful if my ideas are shaped by the purposes of God. "There are many plans in a man's heart, Nevertheless the Lord's counsel – that will stand" (Proverbs 19:21).

"And we know that all things work together for good to those who love God, who [have been] called according to his purpose" (Romans 8:28, NKJV).

My generation needs what my life can produce. God has placed me in this moment in history to accomplish his purposes. "And who knows but that you have come to royal position for such a time as this?" (Esther 4:14).

MOSES' LIFE
(Exodus 3:10): What does God's revelation of His purpose do to Moses' life in the wilderness?

WHERE THIS BLOCK IS IN MY LIFE
What I *know* God wants to do with my life:

What I *sense* God may be trying to do with my life:

BUILDING BLOCK 2 — A SENSE OF SELF

"Of all the judgments that we pass in life, none is as important as the one we pass on ourselves; for that judgment touches the very center of our existence.

"We stand in the midst of an almost infinite network of relationships: to other people, to things, to the universe. And yet, at three o'clock in the morning, when we are alone with ourselves, we are aware that the most intimate and powerful of all relationships and the one we can never escape is the relationship to ourselves. . . .

"At each step of the way, we . . . confront some form of the question, Shall I honor or shall I betray the self? Not that we necessarily identify the issue in these terms; in fact, we rarely do. . . . But in the natural course of our development, we inevitably face a variety of questions that bear on the same ultimate alternatives:·

"Do I belong to myself or to others? Is the primary purpose of my self the pursuit of my own happiness and the fulfillment of my own positive potentialities, or is it compliance with the wants and expectations of others?

"Do I live by my own vision of things or by the vision of others? Is my basic concern with my own approval or with the approval of others?

"Am I to rely chiefly on my own mind or on the minds of my parents or teachers, leaders or guru?"
From Nathaniel Branden, *Honoring the Self*

While Dr. Branden does not factor God into his questions, he asks a central question we must face: Shall I honor or shall I betray my self? God created all of us for a purpose. He designed us with that purpose in mind, and we need to honor the self that God has created. We have to know who we are and have an accurate assessment – a "sober judgment" (Romans 12:3) – of our strengths and weaknesses.

Honoring the self that God created for His purposes is a critical building block

in the foundation of your manhood. Too many African American men grow up being taught to honor everything white, everything not us. We don't value ourselves enough to get all the education we need to fulfill God's purposes for our lives. We often do not make full use of our potential as human beings. We believe the lies and delusions the Domination System has taught us about ourselves.

Moses, as we have seen, started life with a sense of himself as great, as a commander, a leader, a prince, a deliverer. But then after his failure to rescue his people, for 40 years he saw himself as a failure, as inadequate. His sense of self was wrapped in shame and colored with self-doubt and, perhaps, self-hate. He ran to Midian where people accepted him and valued him. He stayed there because he didn't value himself enough to go back and fulfill his God-given purposes. But God put a new sense of self in Moses. Whereas before, Moses had seen himself as isolated, alone, a failure, inadequate – the new building block was a sense of himself as powerful, adequate, full of purpose because God was with him. He came to understand that he was not alone.

Modern psychology has re-learned what the Bible has shown us from ancient times, that a man can't do anything great for God until he has reached a point of honoring himself. A man has to have a strong – or what we call a "cohesive" – sense of self. That is, he can't be divided within himself. "A double minded man is unstable in all his ways" (James 1:8, KJV). This "cohesive self" is when you know and value who you are and you live out who you are in every situation. When psychologists assess a man's sense of self, there are four broad categories we often use to see how far a man has come in developing a cohesive self (see charts on following pages):

COHESIVE SELF	NEUROTIC SELF	BORDER-LINE SELF	PSYCHOTIC SELF
When you experience disappointment in people, yourself, or some other kind of life stress, you remember who you are, what your values are, what your goals are, what your strengths are, and you are not knocked off the path. Sometimes, you may doubt yourself, and you will certainly make mistakes and have regrets; but you will soon recover your vitality, your joy, your sense of purpose, and your sense of comfort with yourself. And you will keep on going.	Because deep down you have some real doubts about yourself and some real confusion about who you are, what your values are, how valuable and lovable you are to people, what your goals are, etc., you develop "neurotic" hang-ups which make life a bit more difficult for you. For example, you may be very sensitive to criticism. You get defensive because your self-esteem is fragile. Or you may turn to another woman to shore up your male ego. Or you may not go back for the education you need.	You have severe confusion about who you are. Deep down you have severe self-hate and a feeling of emptiness. Because of this, you may manifest three major behavior patterns: • You always avoid. You never allow yourself to get close, to be needy, to be vulnerable, or to show a soft side. You are very defensive. You are a real loner. • You always cling. You cannot tolerate being alone, so you always maintain a close relationship in which the other person may feel smothered, or at least that they have to "mother" you.	You are massively out of touch with who you are and with reality. You have hallucinations, delusions, paranoid thoughts, etc. This is a serious mental illness.

COHESIVE SELF	NEUROTIC SELF	BORDER-LINE SELF	PSYCHOTIC SELF
Because you are secure in who you are, you can allow others to be who they are while at the same time investing deeply in their lives, loving them as they need to be loved. You can be open and vulnerable with people as well because you accept your human weaknesses and can tolerate occasional shame and guilt.	Or you may be a perfectionist, unable to tolerate any failure in yourself or others. Or you may not share your feelings easily, because you have a hang-up about being "weak". These are hang-ups that don't destroy your life, but they make it worse; and it shows that you are not as clear (cohesive) as you need to be on who you are.	Your doubts about yourself make it very difficult for you to step into a leadership role where you will be "out there on a limb." • You always fight. You see people (often subconsciously) as threats to your fragile sense of self, so you attack. You put people down. You make people feel you are superior. You seem cold, distant, untouchable, haughty.	

BUILDING BLOCK 2

HOW DOES GOD PUT THIS BLOCK IN PLACE?

SENSE OF SELF

God designed me with His purpose for me in mind. Therefore, I am the way I am because of why I am. He built into me all the basic characteristics and potential I need to fulfill my purpose.

I am perfect for my purpose. I don't ever need to compare myself with other men or try to be like other men because each of us is needed. "Now the Body is not made up of one part but of many. . . . If the whole body were an eye, where would the sense of hearing be? If the whole body were an ear, where would the sense of smell be? But in fact God has arranged the parts in the body, every one of them, just as he wanted them to be" (I Corinthians 12:14, 17-18).

I should therefore try to have an accurate assessment of who I am and what gifts and potential God has placed into me. "Do not think of yourself more highly than you ought, but rather think of yourself with sober judgment, in accordance with the measure of faith God has given you. . . . We have different gifts, according to the grace given us. . ." (Romans 12:3, 6).

MOSES' LIFE
(Exodus 3:11-12):

Moses' Question (Exodus 3:11):

God's Answer (Exodus 3:12):

WHERE THIS BLOCK IS IN MY LIFE
List some of your major personality traits. (Begin by saying "I am. . ." or "I like. . ." or "I tend to. . . ." Then say how God uses those traits to accomplish his purposes.

Trait   How God Uses It

1. I _____

2. I _____

3. I _____

4. I _____

5. I _____

"Who Am I?" My General Self-Concept: Describe your general sense of who you are.

BUILDING BLOCK 3 — A SENSE OF AUTHORITY

"The greatest power you possess is the power to choose your course in life and to choose your response to whatever happens to you. This is the true meaning of the word responsibility – "response-ability," the ability to choose your response.

"Using a computer metaphor, we could say that you are the programmer, not the program. You are the product of your choices and your decisions, not of your conditions or conditioning. Genes, environment, and childhood can powerfully influence you, but they do not determine you.

"Proactivity means acting based on your values rather than reacting based on emotion or circumstance. It comes from knowing that you are not your thoughts, your feelings, or your moods. You can stand mentally and emotionally apart from these things and choose the actions that best ex-press your values. Eventually, through the process of becoming proactive, you create many of the circumstances in your life." Stephen Covey

Covey pictures it as follows. The outside Circle of Concerns encompasses everything about which we are concerned, everything that touches us, everything that matters to us. The inner Circle of Influence includes what lies within our power to change or determine. As they become more proactive, Covey says, highly effective people discover that they can control or at least influence more and more of the things that concern them.

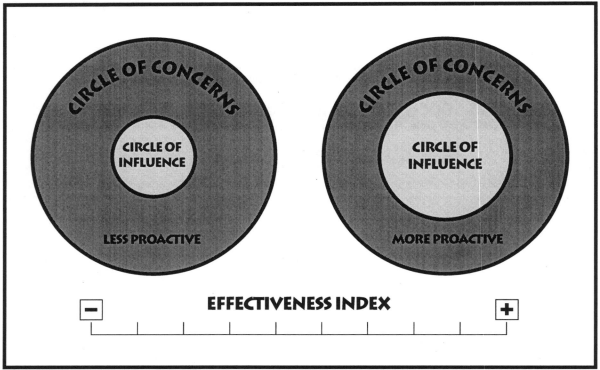

This matches the biblical concept of authority, which we looked at before. When God created humankind, He gave us the dominion or authority over the world and all of life. Because of the Fall, that authority has been given over to the Prince of the world, the Domination System which seeks to control our lives. We saw how Moses had too great a sense of authority, one that did not match his real authority. His authority came from Pharaoh; but when he sought to oppose Pharaoh, he immediately lost that authority. We also saw how many of us have too little a sense of authority.

We are called as men of God to re-seize that authority over the world and especially over our own lives and families. This is what it means to be an adult – accepting responsibility in the areas which God has entrusted to us.

God took this broken man Moses and gave into his hands the responsibility to free the children of Israel. "Now you go," God told him. Moses wanted to know what his authority was, and God told him. Do you know your authority?

| BUILDING BLOCK 3 | HOW DOES GOD PUT THIS BLOCK IN PLACE? |

SENSE OF AUTHORITY

Spiritual: Spiritual authority is to see ourselves as God-sent, God-directed, and God-empowered. This has psychological and social results.

Psychological: Psychologically, we move out of the authority of our family and take our place as adult men, able to make our own decisions as wisely as we can under God's leading.

Social: Socially, we expand our circle of influence so that we help people decide to move in the direction God is leading them. We don't just watch things happen. Under God's anointing, we make them happen. We don't dominate others, preventing them from making up their own minds. Rather, through serving others and loving them as Christ loved, we empower them to hear God for themselves and decide to follow His leading.

MOSES' LIFE
(Exodus 3:13-15, 4:1-9):

Moses' Concerns	God's Answer
1. 3:13	3:14-15
2. 4:1	4:2-9

WHERE THIS BLOCK IS IN MY LIFE

Spiritual: How God-sent and God-directed do I feel?

Psychological: How able am I to decide for myself and act assertively on my decisions?

Social: How effective am I in influencing my circle of people without dominating or manipulating them?

BUILDING BLOCK 4 — A SENSE OF COMPETENCE

The roots of a sense of competence go back to childhood. Through tens of thousands of experiences of trying various things over the years, two things happen:

• We develop certain competencies (abilities) which we use on our jobs, at home, in church, etc.

• We form conclusions about our competencies. We develop a feeling of mastery or a feeling of inadequacy, depending on what we have concluded.

The Bible teaches that God has given all who are His children certain gifts to use in building up His Body and advancing His kingdom in the world. Do we know what those spiritual gifts and natural abilities are? How do we feel about them? Do we feel confident using them, or do we hide from greater responsibility because we

are afraid of embarrassing ourselves? Perhaps we are overconfident.

I consistently plant the seeds of greatness within my son's subconscious by telling my son that he is a Prince. He must display the highest character, integrity, and intelligence befitting one of royal heritage. I tell him that being a Prince requires him to maintain a certain standard of behavior and code of conduct. I never confront or challenge him on things that I don't feel are important enough for discipline. I never tell him not to do something or to stop doing something unless I'm prepared to discipline him (not necessarily by spanking) if he doesn't respond immediately. And finally, I make it a point to acknowledge and reward good behavior and never to allow unacceptable behavior to go uncensored!

Mychal Wynn, *Empowering African-American Males to Succeed*

Moses had to wrestle with his own feelings of inadequacy. God had to put the building block of self-confidence back into the foundation of this once supremely confident man. Perhaps you, too, need this building block shored up or replaced.

44

BUILDING BLOCK 4

SENSE OF COMPETENCE

Feeling of Mastery
This is how much I feel competent, able to master the tasks of my life. This is my own subjective sense of my abilities and gifts, of my effectiveness in life.

Actual Mastery Level
This is how much I actually master the tasks of my life. I may feel more competent than my performance suggests. Or I may feel less competent than my performance warrants. Paul tells us to assess ourselves neither too high nor too low (Romans 12:3).

HOW DOES GOD PUT THIS BLOCK IN PLACE?

MOSES' SELF-DOUBT
(Exodus 4:10):

How deep is it?

God's Response?

WHERE THIS BLOCK IS IN MY LIFE

Things I Do Often: When I Do This, I Tend To Feel:

	Confident	Unsure of Myself	Incompetent
1.	○	○	○
2.	○	○	○
3.	○	○	○
4.	○	○	○

BUILDING BLOCK 5 — A SENSE OF CONNECTION

Have you ever noticed how difficult it is for men to get close and open up to people? All humans start out life close to our mothers. But unlike girls, who must identify with their mothers to become women, boys have to focus on how they are different from their mothers if they are to become men. More and more, to affirm their masculine identity, they must focus on how unlike mother they are. They must separate from her and identify with father (if he's there). Yet this separation happens at a time when they still yearn as much as girls to be close to mother. Thus, their desire for closeness feels like weakness, "girlish", makes many men feel like a "mama's boy", often leading to feelings of shame. They want to be close, but to be a boy they feel they must separate. They want hugs, but to be a boy they must pretend that they don't need them. They want to be soft and cry sometimes, but they struggle with ambivalence about how masculine it is to be so like mother – soft.

When such men grow up, what they express openly, overtly is their quest for independence, toughness, etc. But covertly, behind the mask, there is another side of the men, the side that wants connection.

How do men express this hidden side to them? One way is what I call the "saving face" strategy.

THE SAVING FACE STRATEGY

Dr. Samuel Osherson, a long-time observer of men, has suggested (in *Wrestling with Love*) that men use strategies for connecting with women and others which preserve their self-esteem at all costs. These strategies very often seem like attempts to disconnect, but in fact are a way for men to connect without admitting that we feel needy. (Who, me? Needy? Shame, shame, shame!)

Aggression. Men use aggression frequently to maintain connection in important relationships without admitting it. They may have learned early in relationships with their father, with other boys, or with teachers that the way to get attention was to put a little life into relationships through aggression of some kind. I recently conducted a coed counseling group composed of older teenagers. Every time painful emotions were expressed in the group – usually by the girls – several of the boys would blurt out teasing-type jokes. While such jokes can often be seen as attempts to lower the

emotional temperature, they can also be seen as the boys' attempts to connect with the hurting girls. They were attempting to make them feel better, but in a way that did not expose the boys' own pain.

At a recent seminar, I separated the men from the women and asked each group to talk about what their gender needed and how they go about getting their needs met. The women displayed many of the classic patterns of female communicating, including expressing fairly intimate things about their own yearnings and struggles. The men, on the other hand, were much more theoretical and general in their discussion, even going so far as drawing up a chart of their needs and strategies – another classic male communication pattern! But they also taunted and teased each other in a good-natured (yet covertly aggressive) way. It was the only way the men could "get real" with each other in their generally abstract discussion. It allowed them to be real without exposing their shame and vulnerability. Says Dr. Osherson,

> We often make the mistake of assuming that men love sports because of their aggressive, competitive needs. But on the football field, at fraternity hazings, in the law school class or factory assembly line, as well as in corporate offices, the assertion of toughness allows men to feel tender. On the football field a brawny fullback plows into the line and a bunch of sweaty, beefy men tromp all over each other. Yet when the play ends, the players put their arms around each other, pat each other, and often express deep affection out of the shared pain and sacrifice of their bodies. . . . Most male rites of passage, when they exist at all, are organized around some affirmation of the ability to endure pain and display toughness. These rituals allow for tenderness and care, even as they disavow it by reminding us of toughness and mastery. *(Wrestling with Love)*

Anger. When things get too intimate, too threatening, a typical male ploy is to provoke a fight. Fighting is one way of staying emotionally connected while also feeling strong rather than vulnerable. Men are often much more comfortable revealing anger than revealing the hurt and shame that usually underlies the anger. The woman's reaction may be to feel distanced by the anger; but for the man it is often not only a distancing ploy but also a face-saving way of expressing the feeling that the woman has penetrated past his exterior to affect his inner self.

Boasting. This was Joseph's strategy. No doubt he felt pretty alienated from his brothers already because of his exalted position in the family and his special robe. Wanting to connect with them, to share his dreams with them, he tells them his dreams. However, he appears to them to be grandiose and "ego-tripping", play-

ing a "one-upmanship" number on them. They miss his yearning to connect, and – typical of males – respond to the dominance message in Joseph's dreams. "Do you think you're going to rule over us, you little upstart pip-squeak?" they ask him in effect.

Men often clumsily try to share their hopes and dreams with each other and with women, but it often comes out in a boasting, even macho, way that protects their self-esteem in case the other person doesn't affirm their dreams or, worse, puts them down.

Dance Away Loving. Family therapists are very familiar with the dances couples do over closeness and distance. What they have discovered is that for most couples, there is a balance between closeness and distance, one with which they are both comfortable. One member of the couple, usually the wife, carries more of the desire for closeness. The other member, usually the husband, expresses more of the desire for distance. Both of them need closeness and space, but they are each more in touch with one need or the other.

Consequently, what happens is that the spouse feeling a need for closeness pursues the distancer. The distancer then moves away, which causes the pursuer to try even harder to close the distance, at first through positive means but eventually through anger and demands. This becomes their dance. She dances closer. He dances away – but not too far away! He doesn't actually leave the relation-

ship. Covertly, he needs her to maintain the relationship, needs her to get them to relate and to talk. And therein lies the key to the solution.

Therapists usually advise the pursuer to stop pursuing and start getting in touch with her own need for space and her ability to do other positive things. This tactical change often causes the distancer to feel neglected and forces him to get in touch with his own need for closeness. For an excellent work on this topic, see Napier's *The Fragile Bond.*

Sex. Dr. Barbara DeAngelis suggests (in *Secrets About Men Every Woman Should Know*), that often men express their needs for connection while saving face through sex.

> Often a man will feel disturbing emotions building up inside him. Perhaps he's worried about a project he's working on. Perhaps he just had a conversation with one of his elderly parents and is feeling sad at having to face their physical and mental deterioration. Perhaps he's feeling guilty for the insensitive way he treated you earlier. . . . Most men aren't brought up to feel that it is okay to express vulnerable feelings like fear, hurt, helplessness, confusion, disappointment, regret. So either your partner won't feel safe expressing these feelings verbally, or he won't know how to.

And suddenly, he's in the
mood for sex.

In fact, DeAngelis states that a man feels
emotionally rejected when the woman in
his life rejects his sexual advances. "When
your partner makes a sexual overture to
you," she advises women, "he is doing
more than asking for sex. He is saying,
'Please accept me; please receive me.'"
(p. 134)

God was telling Moses to go be a hero
(in a way). If Moses had been the typical
male, he might have gone without being
honest about his feelings of being out on
a limb all by himself. Instead, he was
honest with God about his need for connection, his need for human support;
and God met him. How honest are you
about your need for connection? Do you
use any of the face saving strategies men-
tioned above? To explore where you are
in your need for connection, complete
the following exercise.

BUILDING BLOCK 5

SENSE OF CONNECTION

Past

I know my roots, the people I come from. I know the strengths I receive because I come from them.

Present

I know who I belong to today. I know who is traveling with me, who accepts me and supports me in my journey as a man. I know who is helping me become what God purposed for me to be. I do not feel alone.

HOW DOES GOD PUT THIS BLOCK IN PLACE?

MOSES' LIFE

Moses' Sense of Belonging:	God's Answer:
1. 2:22	3:6
2. 4:13	4:14-16

- -

WHERE THIS BLOCK IS IN MY LIFE

The People in My Roots:	Strengths I Get From Them:
My Present Community:	Strengths I Get From Them:

Strategies I Use to Hide My Need for Connection:

Step Three — Reconnect

We have examined how men like Moses and ourselves get broken through the outer Domination System and an inner "hero quest" that often fails. And we have also looked at how God recovers us from our "Midian" hiding places and rebuilds the foundation of our lives as men.

Now we are ready to look at how we can help reconnect boys to their God-given purposes. The Domination System has done everything possible to destroy black boys' sense of purpose. We must challenge that System and engage the Principalities and Powers in a no-holds-barred struggle for the souls and manhood of our boys.

We find an example of how to wage such a struggle from the life of Moses. When he finally went back to Egypt, he found his own people deeply discouraged and depressed. They had no sense of pur-

pose. The Domination System in Egypt had broken them. They were very similar to many of our boys, even to the point of fighting among themselves.

Moses had to reconnect them to the purposes of God which He first spoke to Abraham concerning the nation of Israel. This was not easy for Moses, nor will it be easy for us. The Domination System will fight us to the death. But we can win if we learn the important lessons of Reconnection.

This section examines the biblical model for reconnecting people oppressed by a Domination System. And then we look at some specific ways in which you as a man can reconnect boys to God's purposes through effectively fathering and/or mentoring – especially through sharing your wisdom.

PURSUING GOD'S PURPOSE

EXODUS 4 - 6

Moses' outer world broke him 40 years earlier because of an inner vulnerability of which he hadn't been aware. Now God has recovered Moses and is well on the way to rebuilding his foundation. Moses is ready – sort of – to face Egypt again, with all of its challenges.

Pursuing God's purpose for our life will require our recovery and the rebuilding of our foundation before we are ready to move out with power into whatever Egypt He selects. We need to be sensitive to his timing, so that we do not move before we are ready – as Moses did at first. But when God reveals His timing to us (it is usually after he has begun to put in place those basic building blocks), then we are going to have to learn how to pursue God's purposes in the face of fierce opposition by the Principalities and Powers. Similarly, we are going to have to learn how to help our boys pursue God's purposes.

UNDERSTANDING THE CHALLENGE

Moses found the Hebrews deeply discouraged and feeling hopeless. This is what happens when men and boys live under the Domination System without someone to help them cope. This is why, Professor Wink says, we must focus not only on the outer structures that oppress us as black men and boys, but also on our own internal sense of oppression and powerlessness:

> Besides an unmasking of the oppressors, there must also be a healing of the servile will in their victims. . . . Simply criticizing the illegitimacy of the masters can lead to two results, both of them negative. The oppressed may decide to beat the oppressors at their own game, rather than changing the game. . . . Or the recognition . . . (that they have allowed themselves to be dominated by their oppressors) may foster self-doubt: If I have been so cowardly and stupid as to put up with such treatment, I deserve what I get. It is my own fault that I am weak. . . . The victims blame themselves, and the system gets off unscathed.

What do we do about this sense of powerlessness when we find it in ourselves or in the boys we are trying to nurture to manhood? Professor Wink has a suggestion:

> A sense of powerlessness is always a spiritual disease deliberately induced by the Powers to keep us complicit (submissive). Any time we feel powerless, we need to step back and ask, What Principality or Power has me in its spell? No one is ever completely powerless. Even if it is only a matter of choosing the attitude with which we die, we are never fully in the control of the Powers unless we grant them that power. . . . The victory of faith over the Powers lies not in immunity to their wrath, but in emancipation from their delusions. And as to their wrath, even then we do not know the limits of God's redeeming grace. So it is always appropriate to pray for miracles. What seems to us impossible is usually another's limited vision or faithlessness

in which we have let ourselves become trapped. . . .

Those who have internalized their oppression, who are awed by the Beast (Satan) and its powers into passive obedience and who worship its show of might, provide it all the permission it needs continually to extend its power. . . . Liberation from negative socialization and internalized oppression is a never-completed task in the discernment of spirits. To exercise this discernment, we need eyes that see the invisible. To break the spell of delusion, we need a vision of God's domination-free order (the kingdom of God) and a way to implement it. For that, we look to God's new charter for reality, as declared by Jesus.

Wink, *Engaging the Powers*

This is what Moses did. He came to a people who were "awed by the Beast and its powers (Egypt) into passive obedience." Later, in the desert, while Moses was on the mountain with God, the people persuaded Aaron to make a golden calf, one of Egypt's gods. They felt insecure and afraid without their masters to provide for them and tell them what to do. They had internalized their own oppression.

Moses' task was to free them not only from their external oppression but also from their own sense of powerlessness. Similarly, our task as African American men, on the one hand, is to free ourselves and our boys from all the external structures that hurt us (such as poor schools, poor job opportunities, lack of fathers or other adult male role models, and gangs). On the other hand, our task is also to free ourselves and our boys from our inner powerlessness and hopelessness, from our willingness to believe the world's delusions and bow our knees before the world's gods.

How do we engage these Powers and reconnect our boys and ourselves to God's purposes? Let's look at how Moses did it.

THE RECONNECTION PROCESS

STEP 1
Promoting Spiritual Discernment (Exodus 4:29-31; 6:9).

What did Moses do to free his people from their inner domination? (Hint: What was the vision he gave them?)

- -

RECONNECTION PRINCIPLE
What characteristics do you have that will help a boy "see the invisible," see what God is trying to do in his life? (Don't focus on what you will TELL him, but on what through your life you can SHOW him.)

In what ways do you bring people together behind a vision? In what ways do you cause conflicts and division?

- -

STEP 2
Finding and Getting to the Root of the Problem (Exodus 5:1).

By whom was the whole Egyptian Domination System maintained?

Why, then, did Moses and Aaron go straight to that person?

Get to the Root.

A PROBLEM YOU FACE
Describe briefly a problem you face.

A PROBLEM A BOY FACES
Describe briefly a problem a boy you know faces.

ROOT OF THE PROBLEM
Ignore the symptoms and consequences of your problem. What are the root causes? Be specific. (Don't just say "sin" or "pride".) Be concrete. What do you do? What feelings are at the heart of your problem? What underlying attitudes or misperceptions?

ROOT OF THE PROBLEM
Ignore the symptoms and consequences. What are the root causes? Be specific.

WHAT YOU CAN DO
"No one is ever completely powerless," says Dr. Wink. What is in your power – your circle of influence – to do about the root of your problem?

WHAT YOU BOTH CAN DO
What is in your power – your circle of influence – to do about the root of the boy's problem? What is in the boy's power to do?

STEP 3
Hold On to Hope When Vision Dies (Exodus 5:4-6:10)

What happened to the vision Moses had? How did he react? (Look at Exodus 5:22-23.)

THE TYPICAL PATTERN WITH GOD-GIVEN DREAMS

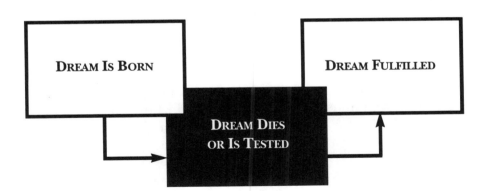

DREAM IS BORN

DREAM FULFILLED

DREAM DIES OR IS TESTED

• Joseph's Dream	• Joseph "dies" (enslaved)	• Joseph's dreams fulfilled
• Elisha's Call	• Elisha serves Elijah for years	• Elisha gets double portion
• Paul's Call	• Paul waits in Tarsus for years	• Paul becomes apostle to the Gentiles; writes Scripture

RECOVERY PRINCIPLE

Look at how God tests your dreams.

A DREAM YOU HAD
Describe a dream you had.

A DREAM A BOY HAD
Describe a dream your boy had or has.

HOW IT DIED OR WAS TESTED
Describe how it died or was tested.

HOW IT DIED OR IS BEING TESTED
Describe how it died or is being tested.

HOW GOD SUSTAINED HOPE
Describe how God kept hope alive.

HOW GOD CAN SUSTAIN HOPE
Describe how God can keep the boy's hope alive through you.

HOW FULFILLED
Describe how God brought your dream to fulfillment.

HOW FULFILLED
Describe how God can use you to bring the boy's dream to fulfillment.

These three principles – discerning what God is doing in our lives, getting to the root of the problems that are dominating us, and learning endurance through holding on to hope in dark times – are very important if we are going to nurture African American boys to manhood in the American Domination System. We have to practice these principles in our own lives and teach them to our boys.

How best can you teach them? By telling them your story, the story you have told in this workbook. If you let boys into your struggles, if you share with them the things you wrote in this workbook about yourself, then you will do a lot to reconnect them to God's purposes. Dr. Robert Akeret calls this "Elder Telling." In *Let the Journey Begin,* our program for boys, we do a lot of Elder Telling. In the next section, I am going to give you a few more suggestions about how you can pass on your life to a boy through telling your life story effectively.

ELDER TALES — RECONNECTING BOYS TO GOD'S PURPOSE

Wisdom is truth that has been lived. It is practical, applied truth because it has come from God through the mouthpiece of a person's life (not just their lips). When we hear wisdom, we can see immediately its application to our lives because it has already been applied in someone else's life.

A man gets wisdom in life through both the highs and the lows of his journey. God teaches him wisdom through his successes, his spiritual victories, his achievements, and the good things that have happened to him. But a man also gains wisdom – or can gain wisdom – through his failures, his sins, his brokenness. This is the power of God's grace that can transform a man as powerfully through his obedience as through his disobedience.

> Transformation is that process of death and rebirth whereby what was our weakness becomes our strength. . . . transformation turns the mess to glory. . . . It is not as though we started from ground zero on a scale of 1 to 10, arrived at point 2 to begin again. It is as though having fallen at 2, we

have returned as the prodigal son at point 7 or more to put on the ring and robe of authority, having gained by what we have been through, wiser and richer than we would have been had we never fallen! . . .

Every wilderness in our personal life becomes part of "the leaves of the tree (that are) for the healing of the nations" (Rev. 22:2). . . . That is the joy of the gospel and the meaning of transformation, not merely return, but fullness of victory for ministry to others.

Grace never says that we should run out to sin in order to become wiser. Rather, as awful as sin is and as much as it is to be deplored, the latter side of it by the foolishness of the gospel is the grace of God to turn every degradation into our highest glory! . . . God forgets our sin, but it is not wisdom or fullness if we do. Having fallen, remembering means we cannot justify blaming another, and we are prepared by our "misbeings" and "misdoings" to help others from the same holes and traps.

. . . Neither healing nor transformation ever erases what is past. That would be to invalidate rather than to celebrate. Transformation says, "For this reason we have lived and sinned and have been redeemed, that out of the ashes of what we have done has grown the ministry we are."

. . . Transformation therefore, confirms that Satan has won no victories whatsoever among the saved, for from the ground plan of creation, even as God planned to turn the lowly cross to highest victory, so He has turned every aspect of our (seemingly) defeated lives to glory.

. . . The formerly depressed know by their own desert experiences how to feed the downtrodden the only kind of manna they can receive. The judgmental become tenderhearted extenders of mercy.

John & Paula Sanford, *The Transformation of the Inner Man*

God takes our brokenness and transforms us into living witnesses of His grace:

> Although I am less than the least of all God's people, this grace was given me: to preach to the Gentiles the unsearchable riches of Christ.
>
> His intent was that now, through the church, the manifold wisdom of God should be made known to the rulers and authorities in the heavenly realms [and their Domination System!] according to his eternal purpose which he accomplished in Christ Jesus our Lord. (Ephesians 3:8-11)

God puts our formerly broken, still-being-rebuilt lives (Philippians 3:12) on display to the principalities and powers as trophies of His transforming grace and power, something He purposed from before the foundation of the world. It becomes the very basis of our ministry:

> Blessed be . . . God . . . who comforts us in all our tribulation, **that we may be able to comfort those** who are in any trouble, **with the comfort with which we ourselves are comforted** by God. For as the sufferings of Christ abound in us, so our consolation also abounds through Christ. Now if we are afflicted, it is for your

consolation and salvation. . . . Or if we are comforted, it is for your consolation and salvation. (II Corinthians 1:3-6, NKJV, emphasis added)

This is a powerful concept. If our suffering was caused by others, on the one hand, it is so that we can minister to fellow sufferers. (You meant it for evil, Joseph told the brothers who had sold him into slavery 22 years previously, "but God meant it for good . . . to save many people alive" (Genesis 50:20, NKJV). On the other hand, if our suffering was caused by ourselves, God will still in His grace forgive us, sanctify us, and use us as ministers of His grace, a testament of His mercy:

> We have this treasure in earthen vessels (ordinary clay pots used in the household which were always chipping and cracking), that the excellency of the power may be of God, and not of us. . . . For all things are for your sakes, that the abundant grace might through the thanksgiving of many redound to the glory of God. (II Corinthians 4:7, 15)

If you believe all this, then you must become an effective witness to God's grace to boys who are in desperate need of mercy and grace, boys who need to be reconnected to God's purpose for their lives. Put another way, you must become an effective story-teller to boys who are hungry for real men – men they can see, touch, and understand – real men who know the power of God's transforming grace, men who have walked not only the mountain tops but also the valleys and have come through to tell of God's love and faithfulness. Boys need real men, and you can be such a man to them.

EVERY PERSON'S LIFE IS WORTH A NOVEL

That's the title of a book written by Irving Polster, a very sensitive psychotherapist. He's right. Your life is worth a novel. But since few publishers are likely to be interested in publishing your story, you must publish it yourself in the ancient African way – through oral story-telling. That is how boys were taught to be men by our forefathers. They were told the stories of the tribe by the tribal elders. Through those stories, they came to understand who they were.

You are now committing yourself to becoming an elder to some boy (your own son or someone else's). One of the most powerful things you can do for that boy is to tell him the tales of your life. Give him a sense of what the journey to manhood is all about. Help him to understand your struggles and your victories, how you handle defeat, and what you do with shame.

If you will believe what I am saying and act on it, it will not be long before you are convinced also about the power of stories in boys' lives. But first you must gather together stories from your life in eight crucial areas in which a boy needs guidance. These eight areas are the character traits and attitudes we try to build into him in Project Manhood. In fact, we have the boys recite these traits in an Oath of Manhood at every Project Manhood meeting. On the next page you will find the Oath. As you read it, begin to think about your own life and what stories you could tell that would illustrate to a boy how to be such a man OR how not to be such a man (your failures will be just as powerful to him as your successes).

After you read the Oath, take a few minutes and jot down in the blank pages at the end of this workbook any memories or stories that come to you about any of the eight traits. This way, you will be able to teach a boy the importance of those traits through your own life's stories. Later, I am going to suggest you do a few more exercises to help you gather your stories together in preparation for telling them.

THE OATH OF MANHOOD
EIGHT ATTITUDES AUTHENTIC MEN HAVE

	ATTITUDE	MEANING	BASIS*
1	I am Teachable	I am strong enough to know that I need help. I need the Lord and I need other people.	Blessed are the poor in spirit, for theirs is the kingdom of heaven.
2	I am Determined	Pain doesn't make me give up. It makes me grow.	Blessed are those who mourn, for they will be comforted.
3	I am a Gentleman	I am assertive like Christ, not aggressive. I always treat everyone with respect.	Blessed are the meek, for they will inherit the earth.
4	I am Principled	I make choices based on my principles and goals, striving for moral integrity & personal excellence.	Blessed are those who hunger and thirst for righteousness, for they will be filled.
5	I am Loving	I try to love others the way that Jesus Christ has loved me, seeking their highest good.	Blessed are the merciful, for they will be shown mercy.
6	I am Open-Hearted & Open-Minded	I am not defensive. I have opened myself deeply to God's truth, and He gives me wisdom in everything I face.	Blessed are the pure in heart, for they will see God.
7	I am a Bridge Builder	I try to understand others and find win-win solutions to problems.	Blessed are the peacemakers, for they will be called children of God.
8	I am a Warrior	I fight for justice & true freedom for my people, with Christ's power pulling down the strongholds that hold them captive.	Blessed are those who are persecuted because of righteousness, for theirs is the kingdom of heaven.

! I AM AN AFRICAN AMERICAN MAN OF GOD.

*Taken from Matthew 5:3–10.

64

One final note about Elder Tales. Don't try to tell all your stories at once. Look for teachable moments as you spend time with your boy – moments when it will be natural for you to bring out a story and tell him. Perhaps the subject will come up naturally during your time together. If not, in the *Let the Journey Begin* curriculum, there are scheduled times when we ask the men to tell their tales about certain topics.

But even on an informal basis, as you spend time with a boy, there will be many opportunities to tell him the tales of your life that will illustrate and drive home the wisdom you have learned, especially in the eight character areas of the Oath of Manhood. I encourage you to memorize that Oath as we ask the boys to do, and then look for opportunities to teach it to your boy through your own life example.

GATHERING YOUR LIFE'S WISDOM

In the exercises below, you will gather some of the stories which will help you reconnect boys to God's purpose for their lives. Your focus here is not on teaching them the Bible per se, but rather showing them how the God of biblical men and women has been active in your own life, teaching you through your successes and your failures.

If you are doing this in a group, I suggest you do these exercises as homework, then come back and share some of your stories with the rest of your group as dramatically as you can. This will knit you closer together as men and will allow you to practice your story-telling before you tell it to boys.

STEPPINGSTONES

The Steppingstones exercise asks you to think back over the course of your life and list the ten or so key events which you consider to be most meaningful in the unfolding of your life. Don't analyze. Just sit quietly, breathe deeply, and allow your mind to wander over your life's journey. What events – external or internal – stand out as you reflect back over your life? What were the moments that most shaped you as a man, a person, a Christian? Breathe deeply, relax, and let your mind wander. See the people who were at those steppingstone periods. Feel the feelings. Let your mind re-live the experiences, and then write down each steppingstone with a few phrases. Don't try to write everything now. Just jot down a few phrases or sentences that will remind you of what happened.

Now that you have your list, you can go back over your phrases/sentences and fill in the details, either on paper or in your mind (better to do it on paper). Try to turn each steppingstone into a brief (3- to 5-minute) story that would help a boy understand what happened to you at that particular period of your life and why it stands out to you as something that helped shape you into the man you are.

TURNING POINTS

This exercise is taken from Dr. Robert Akeret's *Family Tales, Family Wisdom: How to Gather the Stories of a Lifetime and Share Them with Your Family*. I strongly recommend that you buy that book and study it.

The Turning Points exercise is different than the Steppingstones exercise in that steppingstones are more general whereas this exercise asks you to think of the events that made your life change direction. There may be some overlap between your steppingstones – the inner and outer events that made you who you are – and the points at which your life changed direction; but they won't all be the same.

In every person's life, there are critical points that, from that moment onward, alter the course of his or her life. Usually, these turning points are precipitated by a crisis. A decision has to be made. You have to declare who you are and what you want in order to move on. And, by action or default, you do move on. Now, looking back, you can see that this was a turning point in your life, that the way you responded to that crisis defined who you are.

Often these turning points involve dilemmas – whether to stay with someone or to leave him, whether to change the way you are living or not to. It may ultimately be your sense of self that is at stake at this critical point – what you stand for, who or what you identify with, what makes your life worth living. . . .

In every life, there are painful turning points – a marriage or love affair that ends, a friendship that is betrayed, a job that is lost, an illness or handicap that takes its toll – and from that point on, nothing in life is ever quite the same again. Yet looking back from the perspective of age, an elder can often see how these painful turning points were a natural part of his life's development, that they provided opportunities for him to change and grow and to define himself in new ways.

Robert Akeret,
Family Tales, Family Wisdom

Now take some time and write in the Notes section (p.68) a few of the turning points in your life. It would be helpful to the boys if you recalled why you acted as you did. Be sure to include at least one painful turning point. What have you learned from your turning points?

THE HERO WITHIN

In this exercise, your task is to identify your own hero quest. In what ways have you tried to be a hero? What have you attempted to achieve in your life? What have your goals been, your hopes and dreams? Have you reached them? Why or why not? List several dreams you have had for your life.

You don't want to communicate a list of goals to boys. So, for each dream you must think about a story that you can tell that will let a boy know what the dream you had was and what happened with it. Remember, make the story interesting, dramatic. Fill in the details.

These three exercises, plus your stories about the eight Oath of Manhood traits, will give you plenty of stories to tell a boy. Your stories will connect him powerfully with you and with the God who has a purpose for your boy's life. In Project Man-

hood, we find the boys listen very closely when older men tell their stories. The boys are hungry for it. It gives them a window into manhood that no woman can provide, no matter how much she loves them. A woman can tell a boy how to be a man. But only a man who is willing to get real can show him. The best way to show him is to open up the window of your life through telling him what has happened in your life – the highs and the lows – and what wisdom you gained from both kinds of experiences.

NOTES

_____

_____

_____

_____

_____

_____

_____

_____

_____

_____

_____

LEADER'S GUIDE

LEADER'S GUIDE

This section is for those who are leading the group discussion. It contains some general suggestions about leading discussions and gives some answers to the Bible study portions of the manual. It also has suggested readings for working with males.

If you are a member of a group, DO NOT READ THIS SECTION. The whole point of this workbook is to help you discover for yourself what God is saying in His Word. If you are not a member of a group but you are doing this workbook on your own, then read this section only after you have completed a particular Bible study.

These answers are NOT inspired of God. They are the author's understanding of Scripture. Only the Holy Spirit can give you the true answers, although I trust that your spirit will witness to my spirit regarding what God is saying to us.

This workbook is best used in a weekly or every other week format. Meeting only once a month will allow the men to forget what they learned during their last session. This problem is compounded for those men who miss a session. You can also use this workbook powerfully in an overnight retreat format.

We have found these discussions to be powerful. They bring out some deep insights into Scripture and encourage men to open up their lives more than they ever have to another man. The thing I have heard men say most about these group discussions is that they are healing.

It is critical that you, the group leader, are an accepting person. If you tend to be judgmental, focusing on what people have done wrong and pointing it out to them, please do not try to lead this ministry. You will shut men down, close them up, and turn them off. You will not heal them with a critical spirit. You will increase their sense of shame. I have found – and the Bible supports – that what we need is grace in order to become more righteous. We need God's grace, and we need man's acceptance (Galatians 6:1). Show the men this grace, and they will change. Criticize their behavior or preach to them about what they should be doing, and you will make them hide. Men are good at hiding. This workbook is designed to bring them out

of Midian where they are hiding and reestablish God's purpose in their lives. That can only be done through love and acceptance.

TIPS FOR LEADING GROUP DISCUSSIONS

1. LISTEN FAR MORE THAN YOU SPEAK.
The whole point of this workbook is to help men discover for themselves what God is trying to do in their lives. Get them to talk. Try not to interject comments that stop the men from talking. Avoid responses such as:

• "You'll be fine." (Shuts down their feelings. Makes them feel ashamed.)

• "It's not so bad. Just trust God." (Same problems as above.)

Remember, feelings are not wrong in themselves. It's what we do with them that is right or wrong. Do we let them fester (do we let the sun go down on them); or do we try to resolve them?

2. ASK GOOD FOLLOW-UP QUESTIONS.
Many of the questions you need to ask the men are spelled out in the workbook. But no workbook can cover everything, so you will need to ask follow-up questions. Probe for specifics. Don't be satisfied with the "right," "Christian" answer. Challenge the men. Play devil's advocate and see how deep their faith and understanding really go. Get them to give you examples. Don't play church. That is,

don't be satisfied with nice, pat answers. Try to get down past the scabs to the wounds the men have buried deep inside them.

3. DON'T ANSWER YOUR OWN QUESTIONS.
If the question is not understood, repeat it or rephrase it. If people learn that you will do most of the talking, they will become quiet and passive or lose interest in the sessions.

4. DON'T BE AFRAID OF SILENCE.
Sometimes men need some time to think, to sort out their feelings and thoughts on a subject. Learn to distinguish, however, between the times when people are thinking and when the question is unclear or irrelevant.

5. DON'T BE CONTENT WITH JUST ONE ANSWER.
Other contributions will add depth and richness to the discussion. Ask the others what they think, or ask if anyone has other ideas until several people have had a chance to speak.

6. BE AFFIRMING.
Men will be more willing to contribute if they feel their answers are genuinely

appreciated. Even when you disagree, thank the men for their contributions: "That's a good point." "I never really thought of it that way before." If you disagree, ask a follow-up question rather than telling them they are wrong: "Can you show us where you get that from the text?"

When a man comes up with a better answer than the one you stated, acknowledge how helpful his comment is to the group and to you.

7. STICK TO THE TOPIC UNDER DISCUSSION. Resist the temptation to go after interesting but unrelated ideas. Offer to return to a topic with the group later or in a private conversation with a person who is interested in the new topic.

8. MAINTAIN CONFIDENTIALITY. "What is shared in the group stays in the group," should be your group's motto. Be very, very, very careful, or you will destroy their trust.

COMMON PROBLEMS AND HOW TO HANDLE THEM

1. MEN WHO MONOPOLIZE THE DISCUSSION.

• Examine yourself. Are you monopolizing the discussion?

• Direct questions to specific men so monopolizers can't answer them.

• Encourage monopolizers to share the conversation with leading statements such as, "Let's hear from those who haven't said anything yet."

2. ANSWERS THAT ARE OBVIOUSLY WRONG.

• Don't shame the man who made the comment. Thank him for his answer.

• Try not to contradict the man yourself. Ask what others think.

• As suggested above, ask him how he got that answer from the passage.

SOME SUGGESTED ANSWERS
TO THE BIBLE STUDIES

THE EGYPTIAN DOMINATION SYSTEM
(See page 19)

THE PRESSURES EGYPT USED TO DOMINATE

1. Socioeconomic & Political

*Slavery system.
Took away land, businesses.
Very hard labor—no time for rebellion, little energy for each other.*

3. Family

*Told midwives to kill the sons that were born.
Told the Egyptian people to kill the Hebrew sons.*

4. Family

*The midwives provided support to the families by saving the sons
and lying to Pharaoh.*

2. Socioeconomic & Political

*Family traditions—the Hebrew men had centuries of being the heads of their
homes, so they did not lose their sense of hope and authority very
quickly. Worship of God—for a long while they maintained an active worship life.*

THE SUPPORT GOD PROVIDED TO SUSTAIN

THE FALL OF MOSES

(See page 24)

1. Childhood Upbringing: What effect do you think Moses' being a Hebrew and separated from his parents (raised in a "foster home") had on him? (Consider only Exodus 2 and Acts 7:28.)

It gave him a sense of the Lord God, the God of Abraham, Isaac, and Jacob.
It gave him a sense of being a Hebrew.
It may also have made him feel lonely, cut off from his family and people.
It contributed to his sense of God's calling him to free his people, although we don't know exactly when that call came.

2. What effect do you think Moses' being raised an Egyptian prince had on his psychological mindset? (Hint: Think about his self-esteem and his sense of destiny.)

It gave him a sense of being powerful, in control.
It gave him tremendous self-confidence, boldness, a sense of authority.
It made him used to people doing what he told them.
It made him a man of action and a man of war. (Tradition has it that Moses became a great general in Pharaoh's army, winning a great battle.)

3. What do we learn about the character and mindset of Moses in Exodus 2:11-14 and Acts 7:25?

He was bold, decisive, authoritative, self-confident, and filled with a sense of mission, a sense of destiny.

4. Given his background, what was the psychological impact on Moses of the life crisis (life failure) described in Exodus 2:13-15?

This self-confident man's sense of authority and mission was completely shattered. Rejected by both Egyptians and Hebrews, he fled in disgrace and great confusion. He probably thought to himself, "I thought I was doing God's will." It's one thing to have the bottom drop out if you are doing wrong. It's another to try to do right and still fall!

5. Given everything that had happened to him, why would Moses agree to stay in the Midian desert for 40 years, giving up his hero quest to free his people (Exodus 2:21)? (Hint: Think of what he was running from and what he got from the land of Midian.)

In Midian, he was instantly accepted. He was safe. He could raise a family and a herd and be at peace.

THE RECOVERY OF MOSES

(See page 30)

STEP 1: RESTORING INTEREST

Why does God light a fire (Exodus 3:1-4)?

To get Moses' attention. He didn't get his attention through something negative in his life, but through something positive. That is why Peter tells wives to win their husbands by their lives, because holiness is supposed to be beautiful, attractive.

Recovery Principle: How has God lit a fire in your recovery process?

STEP 2: RESTORING SELF-HONESTY

(Exodus 3:4-5)
Why does God tell Moses to take off his shoes? Given that Moses is a broken man with low self-esteem, why is it important for him to have this kind of crisis over who he is? (Hint: Think about the first step in Alcoholics Anonymous and about the first Beatitude.) Is God rubbing a broken man's face in the dirt, or is there something healing about this?

We might think that since Moses had a severely damaged self-esteem, he should be made to feel better about himself. That is true, but the only way to deal with a festering wound is to open it up and clean it out. God brought Moses to a point of deep self-honesty. The first step of AA is to admit that one is an alcoholic. Moses had to admit his brokenness before God. This kind of confessing is very different than feeling depressed or pitying oneself. This is a manly thing – to be strong enough to admit that you were not the man you thought you were. You failed. You sinned. You blew it. You have a habit, an addiction, something you can't control,

and you stand before a holy God and completely take off all your protection, everything that you use to prop up your self-esteem. To take off your shoes in that culture meant a sign of respect, of admitting that you were the guest, not the master of the house. It is admitting who you are before God. That honest admitting is the first step of healing.

Recovery Principle: What does this teach us about how we men should deal with the shame in our lives? Should we try to hide it? Should we try to hide from it?

We should admit to God and to each other who we are. We may need to admit it to a counselor as well. Men run from their shame. But ALL men have a lot of shame buried inside of them; and we have to open it up and admit our shame. Otherwise, we will do some crazy things to boost our egos and avoid feeling shame.

STEP 3: RESTORING HOPE (Exodus 3:6-9)

Why is it important for Moses to know that God is the God of Moses' fathers? (Hint: Remember that Moses feels like an alien in Midian.)

Moses felt deeply disconnected from his people, severely rejected. God was letting him know that He was the same God.

Why is it important that Moses know what God has seen and heard?

Discouraged men need to know that God cares, that He knows and feels what they feel. So many men have never had a man to give that to them. Fortunately, God will be a Father to the fatherless and a Mother to the motherless.

Why is it important for Moses to know what God has decided to do?

Discouraged men need to know that God is going to do something about it. Men tend to be action-oriented. When they care, they tend to want to do something about a problem. Moses needed to know that God intended to do something about the situation.

Recovery Principle: Where have you lost hope in your own life? How is God restoring it?

STEP 4: RESTORING PURPOSE (Exodus 3:10-14) What is the significance of the fact that God called Moses to His service at a broken time in Moses' life, instead of waiting for him to get his life together first?

We often feel that we have to wait until we are fixed up before God can use us. This is one reason why so many men stay away from church. They feel ashamed to be there. But God wants a broken and contrite spirit, not a superman. Moses tried to serve God at first as a superman. Now he can serve him as a man without his shoes.

After forty years in Midian, what does Moses' question reveal about his psychological mindset?

That his whole sense of identity was one of being a failure. We call that a "shame-based identity." Our sense of who we are is wrapped up in shame. We feel like a failure all over. It is almost as if Moses is saying to God, "Weren't you there when I failed? Don't you know I already tried that and failed and will always fail because I am a failure?"

What is God's answer?

God realized that Moses' identity was shame-based, wrapped in failure, because Moses did not see himself as connected to God. When we feel totally alone, without any support or affirmation, we feel much worse about ourselves. This is even more true when we feel cut off from God. God wanted Moses to start feeling strong again – not as a hero, a lone hero – but as a man of God. A man connected to God. A man with his God walking beside him.

Recovery Principle: How do you feel about God's call on your life, given your inner sense of shame and failure? What objections do you raise when you hear God's call?

(Probe for specifics here.)

What is God's answer to you? How does He make that Real? (Don't settle for the "right" answer. Is this really real to you? Why is it real? How would you answer a boy who says God has abandoned him? What reasons that make sense would you give him?)

BUILDING BLOCK 1	**HOW DOES GOD PUT THIS BLOCK IN PLACE?**

SENSE OF PURPOSE

A sense of what God has created me for. "For we are his workmanship, created in Christ Jesus to do good works, which God prepared in advance for us to do" (Ephesians 2:10).

While I have many ideas about my life, I can only be truly successful if my ideas are shaped by the purposes of God. "There are many plans in a man's heart, Nevertheless the Lord's counsel – that will stand" (Proverbs 19:21).

"And we know that all things work together for good to those who love God, who [have been] called according to his purpose" (Romans 8:28, NKJV).

My generation needs what my life can produce. God has placed me in this moment in history to accomplish his purposes. "And who knows but that you have come to royal position for such a time as this?" (Esther 4:14).

MOSES' LIFE

(Exodus 3:10): What does God's revelation of His purpose do to Moses' life in the wilderness?

Changes it completely. He is no longer content to raise a family and sheep. He is reconnected to something he felt earlier in his life.

WHERE THIS BLOCK IS IN MY LIFE

What I *know* God wants to do with my life:

What I *sense* God may be trying to do with my life:

(See page 40)

BUILDING BLOCK 2

HOW DOES GOD PUT THIS BLOCK IN PLACE?

SENSE OF SELF

God designed me with His purpose for me in mind. Therefore, I am the way I am because of why I am. He built into me all the basic characteristics and potential I need to fulfill my purpose.

I am perfect for my purpose. I don't ever need to compare myself with other men or try to be like other men because each of us is needed. "Now the Body is not made up of one part but of many. . . . If the whole body were an eye, where would the sense of hearing be? If the whole body were an ear, where would the sense of smell be? But in fact God has arranged the parts in the body, every one of them, just as he wanted them to be" (I Corinthians 12:14, 17-18).

I should therefore try to have an accurate assessment of who I am and what gifts and potential God has placed into me. "Do not think of yourself more highly than you ought, but rather think of yourself with sober judgment, in accordance with the measure of faith God has given you. . . . We have different gifts, according to the grace given us. . ." (Romans 12:3, 6).

MOSES' LIFE
(Exodus 3:11-12):

Moses' Question (Exodus 3:11):
Who am I?

God's Answer (Exodus 3:12):
You are someone whose God is with him.

WHERE THIS BLOCK IS IN MY LIFE
List some of your major personality traits. (Begin by saying, "I am. . ." or "I like. . ." or "I tend to. . . ." Then say how God uses those traits to accomplish his purposes.

Trait   How God Uses It

1. I _____

2. I _____

3. I _____

4. I _____

5. I _____

"Who Am I?" My General Self-Concept: Describe your general sense of who you are.

(See page 43)

BUILDING BLOCK 3	HOW DOES GOD PUT THIS BLOCK IN PLACE?

SENSE OF AUTHORITY

Spiritual: Spiritual authority is to see ourselves as God-sent, God-directed, and God-empowered. This has psychological and social results.

Psychological: Psychologically, we move out of the authority of our family and take our place as adult men, able to make our own decisions as wisely as we can under God's leading.

Social: Socially, we expand our circle of influence so that we help people decide to move in the direction God is leading them. We don't just watch things happen. Under God's anointing, we make them happen. We don't dominate others, preventing them from making up their own minds. Rather, through serving others and loving them as Christ loved, we empower them to hear God for themselves and decide to follow His leading.

MOSES' LIFE
(Exodus 3:13-15, 4:1-9):

Moses' Concerns	God's Answer
1. 3:13	3:14-15
Who shall I say sent me?	*I AM, the all-sufficient one. I AM, the eternally existing one. I AM whatever you need me to be.*
2. 4:1	4:2-9

WHERE THIS BLOCK IS IN MY LIFE

Spiritual: How God-sent and God-directed do I feel?

Psychological: How able am I to decide for myself and act assertively on my decisions?

Social: How effective am I in influencing my circle of people without dominating or manipulating them?

(See page 45)

BUILDING BLOCK 4

SENSE OF COMPETENCE

Feeling of Mastery
This is how much I feel competent, able to master the tasks of my life. This is my own subjective sense of my abilities and gifts, of my effectiveness in life.

Actual Mastery Level
This is how much I actually master the tasks of my life. I may feel more competent than my performance suggests. Or I may feel less competent than my performance warrants. Paul tells us to assess ourselves neither too high nor too low (Romans 12:3).

HOW DOES GOD PUT THIS BLOCK IN PLACE?

MOSES' SELF-DOUBT
(Exodus 4:10):

How deep is it?

He has a failure identity as discussed.

God's Response?

WHERE THIS BLOCK IS IN MY LIFE:

Things I Do Often: When I Do This, I Tend To Feel:

	Confident	Unsure of Myself	Incompetent
1.	◯	◯	◯
2.	◯	◯	◯
3.	◯	◯	◯
4.	◯	◯	◯

(See page 50)

BUILDING BLOCK 5

SENSE OF CONNECTION

Past
I know my roots, the people I come from. I know the strengths I receive because I come from them.

Present
I know who I belong to today. I know who is traveling with me, who accepts me and supports me in my journey as a man. I know who is helping me become what God purposed for me to be. I do not feel alone.

HOW DOES GOD PUT THIS BLOCK IN PLACE?

MOSES' LIFE

Moses' Sense of Belonging:
1. 2:22
A stranger in a strange land.

God's Answer:
3:6
I am the God of your people. They still exist, and you're still a part of them.

2. 4:13
Alone, inadequate because he is alone. There is strength in numbers. We all need support.

4:14-16
Sends Moses' brother Aaron.

– · – · – · – · – · – · – · – · – · – · – · – · – · – · –

WHERE THIS BLOCK IS IN MY LIFE

The People in My Roots:

Strengths I Get From Them:

My Present Community:

Strengths I Get From Them:

Strategies I Use to Hide My Need for Connection:

(See page 55)

THE RECONNECTION PROCESS

STEP 1
Promoting Spiritual Discernment (Exodus 4:29-31; 6:9).

What did Moses do to free his people from their inner domination? (Hint: What was the vision he gave them?)

He helped them to "see the invisible," as Walter Wink puts it. He helped them to see past what the Domination System had tried to get them to believe about themselves. Just as God had found him with a failure identity, Moses found his people with a helplessness identity. He helped them to see what God intended to do about their situation.

RECONNECTION PRINCIPLE
What characteristics do you have that will help a boy "see the invisible," see what God is trying to do in his life? (Don't focus on what you will TELL him, but on what through your life you can SHOW him.)

In what ways do you bring people together behind a vision? In what ways do you cause conflicts and division?

STEP 2
Finding and Getting to the Root of the Problem (Exodus 5:1).

By whom was the whole Egyptian Domination System maintained?
Pharaoh.

Why, then, did Moses and Aaron go straight to that person?
To change the system, they had to get to the one who maintained it.

RECOVERY PRINCIPLE

Get to the Root.

A PROBLEM YOU FACE
Describe briefly a problem you face.

A PROBLEM A BOY FACES
Describe briefly a problem a boy you know faces.

ROOT OF THE PROBLEM
Ignore the symptoms and consequences of your problem. What are the root causes? Be specific. (Don't just say "sin" or "pride".) Be concrete. What do you do? What feelings are at the heart of your problem? What underlying attitudes or misperceptions?

ROOT OF THE PROBLEM
Ignore the symptoms and consequences. What are the root causes? Be specific.

WHAT YOU CAN DO
"No one is ever completely powerless," says Dr. Wink. What is in your power – your circle of influence – to do about the root of your problem?

WHAT YOU BOTH CAN DO
What is in your power – your circle of influence – to do about the root of the boy's problem? What is in the boy's power to do?

(See page 57)

THE RECONNECTION PROCESS

STEP 3
Hold On to Hope When Vision Dies (Exodus 5:4-6:10)

What happened to the vision Moses had? How did he react? (Look at Exodus 5:22-23.)

It seemed to die. Things got a lot worse. He became very discouraged and angry at God.

THE TYPICAL PATTERN WITH GOD-GIVEN DREAMS

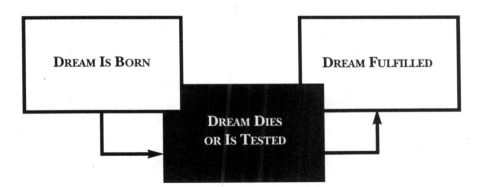

- Joseph's Dream

- Elisha's Call

- Paul's Call

- Joseph "dies" (enslaved)

- Elisha serves Elijah for years

- Paul waits in Tarsus for years

- Joseph's dreams fulfilled

- Elisha gets double portion

- Paul becomes apostle to the Gentiles; writes Scripture

RECOVERY PRINCIPLE

Look at how God tests your dreams.

A DREAM YOU HAD
Describe a dream you had.

A DREAM A BOY HAD
Describe a dream your boy had or has.

HOW IT DIED OR WAS TESTED
Describe how it died or was tested.

HOW IT DIED OR IS BEING TESTED
Describe how it died or is being tested.

HOW GOD SUSTAINED HOPE
Describe how God kept hope alive.

HOW GOD CAN SUSTAIN HOPE
Describe how God can keep the boy's hope alive through you.

HOW FULFILLED
Describe how God brought your dream to fulfillment.

HOW FULFILLED
Describe how God can use you to bring the boy's dream to fulfillment.

REFERENCES & NOTES

Balswick, Jack. *Men at the Crossroads.* Downers Grove, Ill.: InterVarsity Press, 1992.

Betcher, William, and William Pollack. *A Time of Fallen Heroes: The Re-creation of Masculinity.* New York: MacMillan, 1993.

Dalbey, Gordon. *Father and Son.* Nashville: Thomas Nelson, 1992.

Eisenman, Tom. *Temptations Men Face.* Downers Grove, Ill.: InterVarsity Press, 1990.

Gallagher, Vincent. *Three Compulsions That Defeat Most Men.* Minneapolis: Bethany House, 1992.

Hicks, Robert. *Uneasy Manhood.* Nashville: Oliver Nelson, 1991.

Jakes, T. D. *Loose That Man and Let Him Go.* Tulsa: Albany Publishing, 1995.

Kipnis, Aaron. *Knights Without Armor.* Los Angeles: J. P. Tarcher, 1991.

Kunjufu, Jawanza. *Countering the Conspiracy to Destroy Black Boys.* Chicago: African American Images, 1985.

Kunjufu, Jawanza. *Countering the Conspiracy to Destroy Black Boys, Vol. II.* Chicago: African American Images, 1986.

Osherson, Samuel. *Wrestling with Love.* New York: Fawcett Columbine, 1995.

Schaller, James. *The Search for Lost Fathering.* Grand Rapids: Fleming Revell, 1995.

Wilson, Amos. *Black-on-Black Violence: The Psychodynamics of Black Self-Annihilation in Service of White Domination.* New York: Afrikan World InfoSystems, 1990.

Wink, Walter. *Engaging the Powers: Discernment and Resistance in a World of Domination.* Minneapolis: Fortress Press, 1992.

Wink, Walter. *Naming the Powers: The Language of Power in the New Testament.* 1984.

Wink, Walter. *Unmasking the Powers: The Invisible Forces That Determine Human Existence.* Philadelphia: Fortress Press, 1986.

Wynn, Mychal. *Empowering African-American Males to Succeed.* Pasadena: Rising Sun Publishing, 1992.

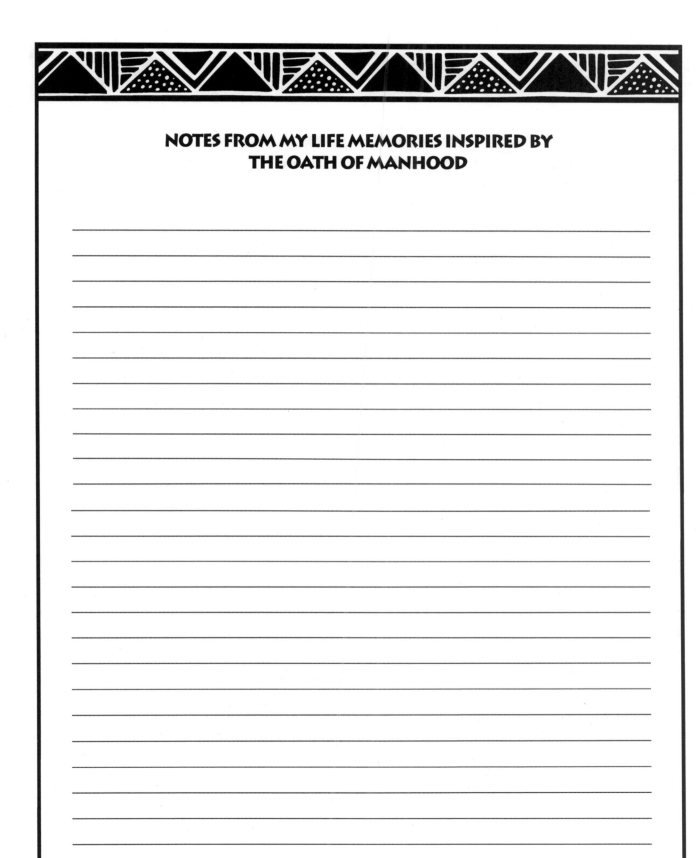

NOTES FROM MY LIFE MEMORIES INSPIRED BY
THE OATH OF MANHOOD

NOTES FROM MY LIFE MEMORIES INSPIRED BY
THE OATH OF MANHOOD

NOTES FROM MY LIFE MEMORIES INSPIRED BY
THE OATH OF MANHOOD

NOTES ON SOME
TURNING POINTS IN MY LIFE